Praise for
Waterfalls, The Moon and Sensible Shoes
ONE LESBIAN LIFE

As an anthropologist, I seek out storytellers whose individual lives can reflect and deepen an understanding of "others" and, in a broader sense, an understanding of the human condition. As one example, Strachan writes about her complicated relationship with Pete interspersed with her own evolving sense of self, using their letters and her journal to document. She fills some entries with the joy of their closeness, while others lay bare an erupting dissonance between them.

—Paul M. Preston, Ph.D. Author of Mother Father Deaf,
Harvard University Press

Engaging and thoughtful! There is a conscious incompleteness to the story; a reflection, perhaps, of the intuitive and sometimes selective ways we write to each other and even to ourselves as Strachan explores moments of her life through personal letters, reflections, and journal entries. And, more to the point, the incompleteness of each of our stories—the ways in which they expand or contract to fit our containers as we, too, grow and change over time. Strachan provides a glimpse into a lifetime of stories well-considered and also, ultimately, open for new ones yet to be woven.

—Hannah Jacobson Blumenfeld, Community-Based Fundraising/
Strategic Project Manager & Board Consultant

The honest, compassionate story told here has many delicious layers beyond just a memoir. The author's rich story telling is greatly enhanced by excerpts from a treasure trove of letters and journals discovered in her parents' possessions. From descriptions of her parents' lives, the reader is treated to a glimpse of the 20th century through the lens of an unconventional background and her father's US Foreign Service assignments in Greece, Pakistan, Sri Lanka, and Vietnam.

—Elizabeth H. Cottrell, writer/blogger,
Hearstpoken.com

A real lesbian writer who loved a gay man? Jill Strachan capably drew me into her beautiful and messy business of growing up and coming out in the 1970s. She captures struggles of knowing oneself, being sexually harassed in her PhD program, and being angrily rejected by her parents after coming out. Know her real lesbian story to understand a piece of the LGBTQ movement. Hurrah for this honest story telling!

—Misti French, member of the Lesbian & Gay
Chorus of Washington, D.C.

Waterfalls, the Moon and Sensible Shoes

ONE LESBIAN LIFE

Jill P. Strachan

Library of Congress Number:

First edition

Book Design by Glen Edelstein, Hudson Valley Book Design,
www.hudsonvalleybookdesign.com

Publishers Cataloging-in-Publication Data TK

978-0-578-99338-6 (Soft cover)
978-0-578-99339-3 (eReaders)

Printed in the United States of America

For Pete, who left early.

NOTE TO THE READER:

Thank you for choosing *Waterfalls, The Moon and Sensible Shoes-One Lesbian Life*. It is not strictly a memoir. Although it draws from that genre, its contents do not follow a chronological order. I have provided time frames to assist. The reader can approach the book in several ways. It is readable from beginning to end. It is also understandable in a pick-and-choose method. Or, read however you wish. I confess I have a habit of reading the beginning of a book and then flipping to the back to read the last page, before proceeding in the normal manner.

As you will see, I have had access to valuable primary sources, including letters and journals from different people. There are many selections from these materials. Most often, I cite the source and date at the end of each excerpt and acknowledge other quotations in footnotes. I have done my best to clarify the author of each but acknowledge that my system might sometimes cause confusion. I have also chosen not to correct some language and words that may startle the 21st century reader. Thank you for your patience and understanding.

Contrary to conventional style guidelines, I have capitalized the words "Lesbian," "Feminist" and related words. I cannot take these words for granted because they have shaped my life.

Jill P. Strachan
October 2021

CONTENTS

Waterfalls, The Moon and Sensible Shoes

ONE LESBIAN LIFE

LOVE BOTTLE

1961

MY FATHER is listening to an Afghan official who is sitting behind a large, metal desk. The man is speaking in English. My mother, my friend Heleen, and I sit quietly nearby in wood chairs. We are at the border between Pakistan and Afghanistan. Midafternoon is upon us in the summer of 1961, and the process of crossing the border cannot be sped up, it can only crawl. My parents are anxious to finish this business and continue the trip to Kabul. They do not want to drive the remaining 130 miles, probably four hours, at night. They know that patience is the only path to getting across the border. We must wait to proceed.

We have just driven through the Khyber Pass, famously known for its mystery and history of intermittent violence, and it is not in any sense a recommended place for a mechanical breakdown or flat tire. All around, standing on outcrops of rock, lone men with guns slung on their shoulders serve as watchmen. The official's office looks down on the two-lane road that carves through the tall mountains.

The official asks questions about our country origin, purpose, and length of visit. He painstakingly writes passport details in an enormous ledger. Heleen's status requires explanation because she is a Dutch citizen traveling with Americans. My father explains that she is my friend whom my parents invited along to keep me company.

We have a *Carne de Passage*, which permits our car to pass into other countries without incurring custom duties. After the official is satisfied with our details, he sits back in his chair; I sense he is looking at Heleen and me. He asks:

How many children do you have, sir?
Two daughters.
Here, we do not like daughters. They are too expensive, so we leave them out on the hills.

My father, whom I lovingly called Daddy, had a gregarious nature that always made him eager for conversation but given the hour and the pressure to continue the drive soon, he does not engage. Plus, the official's words bewilder him, so, setting aside any implied deeper meaning, Daddy resorts to light, awkward laughter in response. He is proud of his two daughters. Shortly after this exchange, we are on our way again.

This trip was memorable for many reasons, but the official's words remained the most remarkable moment of our journey. Their meaning, that women are expendable, has haunted me ever since. I think of that man every time Afghanistan is in the news.

☾   ☾   ☾

This 428-mile road trip from Lahore, Pakistan, where we lived, to Kabul, Afghanistan, was our family vacation when I was 11 and I was happy that Heleen was with us. She hailed from Arnhem, Holland, and she towered over me. We made a funny-looking pair but we got along well.

On our way to Kabul, we stayed for a few days in the lovely, remote Swat Valley, a self-governing, princely state ruled by the Wali of Swat, Miangul Jahanzeb Khan. Unlike Queen Elizabeth II and Prince Phillip, who visited around the same time, we were not overnight guests in the Wali's palace but we had tea with him in his garden. For June, it was chilly.

When we returned from Kabul to Lahore 10 days later, we took an alternate route out of Kabul that Mother had learned about. Always keen to explore the road less chosen, Mother urged us on, despite Daddy's doubts. Her research had not revealed the fact that the road was still under construction in some places, or if she had known, she did not share the information. We found out when we came to a standstill about an hour into the journey when we heard a dynamite explosion up ahead. When the explosions ended, we noticed that the taxi and truck drivers had exited their vehicles and were clearing the road of small boulders and stones that now blocked our way. We joined them and began tossing rocks to the side of the road. Eventually, we returned to our car and resumed the drive but we waited several more times for the road to be cleared. Our careers as road engineers were short-lived.

☾   ☾   ☾

In 1961, in Lahore, Heleen and I socialized with other children of diplomats, foreign service officers, embassy staff, and contractors. We amused ourselves with *Wink 'Em*, a game played in a circle with participants seated in chairs. We also played *Spin the Bottle*, but unlike that game, *Wink 'Em* was subtle and covert. We played it in various spaces even where parents might interrupt unexpectedly. In our version, the premise was to wink at someone you wanted to kiss and then execute.

Wink 'Em was fun but it presented an odd personal challenge. My eyes did not have the requisite muscles for winking because I could only blink them both at the same time. Often, I received either no response from anyone, or two boys would think I meant to wink at them.

Young girls of my acquaintance were not winking at each other in 1961, which was unfortunate for me, because being able to play *Wink 'Em* with girls might have helped with my emerging sexual confusion. I could not wink until I turned 55, and now, at an even older age, when it is acceptable for women to wink at other women, I can manage a wink only after preparatory rehearsal. It is not subtle, however, because I must screw up my face to accomplish the wink, which diminishes the element of surprise. My partner Jane appreciates my effort.

Lahore American School, where I attended, included students from other countries but not Pakistan. My Pakistani best friend was Scheherezade Khan. Our parents introduced us and gently chaperoned our meetings. I enjoyed her company and visited her home and vice versa. Compared to my *Wink 'Em* activities, spending time with Scheherezade was a more sobering application of my free time. As a young Pakistani girl, she could not attend a boy/girl party hosted by an American kid; her future included an arranged marriage. After I left Lahore in September 1961, she wrote to my mother, "Jill and I now write quite regularly to each other; and I hope we shall be able to keep it up always and always." (March 15, 1962). Alas, her beautiful hope did not materialize.

My sister Heather lived with us during her junior year abroad and took classes at the University of the Punjab and Forman Christian College. As an American woman, she could access many opportunities that would not be available to Scheherezade as she grew into her late teen years. Heather was the first woman ever to attend university classes without wearing a veil. Heather was beautiful and she attracted frequent, shy curiosity.

Pakistani men telephoned but if she picked up the receiver and said "hello," they would hang up immediately. She assigned me the responsibility of answering the home phone because the men were less likely to panic if she did not pick up. It was often the case when Heather came to the phone that the caller was no longer there, having lost his nerve. Since she could not socialize individually with her male classmates, Heather would invite a group to our home for tea. This was a command performance for Strachan family members, which was an experience both comical and sad. Mother, Daddy, and I joined Heather in the living room as the men arrived. Conversation would be stilted as Pakistani cultural norms stringently controlled social interactions between unmarried men and women. Usually, one man took the lead in speaking for the others.

My other best friend was Renée Bisbee. She was knowledgeable in the study of boys and love, and she was willing to answer my queries.

Being more mature, she was my primary source of information on my changing body.

> *I have finally gotten hair under my arms. Renée said that it did not mean anything but just before the hair, I got the feeling I was starting my breasts. Maybe not.* (JPS diary, August 6, 1961)

My diary was named Jane but the name bears no connection to my partner Jane, who came into my life almost 40 years later. The diary was a gift from my mother and had a picture of a peppy, blond Girl Scout on its plastic front. I wrote "Hands Off" in pink ink (somewhat faded by the time of this writing) on the front, back, and spine. The diary was equipped with a lock and a tiny key to protect my secrets. I addressed my entries to, "Dear Jane."

It was to Jane that I reported my love for Steve Jung. With Renée's seasoned guidance, I created a secret "love bottle," which I wore on a chain around my neck. It was a small bottle, likely a discarded plastic pill container, which I chose to survive the necessity of sleeping comfortably and to avoid the gaze of peepers. Renée emphasized that I could not remove the bottle except for bathing and swimming; it was a 24/7 commitment. Although the love bottle hung from my neck and was concealed from view under my shirt, Renée assured me that this was the best way of attracting Steve's attention and his love. Extrasensory perception (ESP) would convey the bottle's existence and my love to Steve's heart. Once that happened, she maintained, Steve would notice me.

My mother had a hawk's eye for everything I did. Afraid of what she might see, I was cunning and adept at keeping my secrets. She was ever observant of my neck being grubby when I was a child and, later, of my dirty feet, and finally, on my return visits from college, of my grayish underwear for which she prescribed bleach. These encounters ended in mutual annoyance and anger but her constant attention to my unwashed problems convinced me that cleanliness is an essential component of living a good life.

Steve, the object of my affection, was at least five years older and he did not notice my attention-grabbing attempts. To Jane I confided, *Today, I fixed my bottle. My love note says:*

I love you Steve
I love you Steve
Wherever I go
My heart sings that tune.
Wait, there is more!
It makes me sad to see you sad
And it makes me glad to see you glad
Just remember this simple thing
I love you Steve with all my heart.
Yours, Jill (May 9, 1961)

Sweet, sincere, and my first lesson in unrequited love.

Our time in Lahore was a religious period for me. In contrast to our secular household, I attended church, although not in the company of my parents. Mother had fled her Lutheran upbringing, and Daddy left his English Anglican background when he emigrated to the United States. Together, they settled on Unitarianism, a humanist, liberal faith, which was a natural landing place after their days as socialists in the 1930s and their many votes for the Socialist Party candidate for US president, Norman Thomas. In Lahore, my parents organized monthly gatherings of like-minded Pakistanis, Americans, and others to discuss social issues. This was not appealing to my young mind nor was I invited.

Instead, on Sundays, I would pedal my bike to the Jungs' house along uneven canal paths where bony water buffalo took muddy baths. There, I enjoyed an American pancake breakfast followed by church. Then, I cycled home. This event was my main social engagement with Steve, always in the company of adults. My parents never questioned this behavior but they may have wondered at my motivation to rise early on Sundays.

I find three more references to my love for Steve in my diary. He left Lahore in the summer of 1961. On July 12, 1961, I wrote,

I LOVE Steve very much!

On July 29, my entry was curious and honest:

I don't know whether a girl my age can really tell if she is in love, but I think I do love Steve though I can forget him. . . . I haven't heard from Steve. I wish he would write.

August 16th brought a letter from him.

I heard from Steve today. He didn't say anything much.

After Steve's letter, I knew no more of him. Love was easy come, easy go when I was 11. I soon removed the love bottle and its ragged string from around my neck. The secret of the love bottle remained mine, but I did not shed any tears.

Me with my Duck Willy

UNEXPECTED REUNION

1961, 1980, 2018

ON A sunny Friday in January 2018, I drove to The Plains, Virginia, for lunch. It was an atypical occurrence. For two decades, I had gone to Virginia only when geographically justified, such as traversing the state to get to West Virginia. My personal ban extended to purchases made in Virginia; it would not get my pennies. I tanked up before crossing the state line. Virginia's laws were biased against Lesbian, gay, bisexual, and transgender people. State legislators had carried on massive resistance to the 1954 Supreme Court decision *Brown v. the Board of Education,* which was a major step in ending school segregation. The Supreme Court overturned Virginia's ban on interracial marriage in *Loving v. Virginia* in 1973. These events were seared into my consciousness, and they fueled my boycott of the state of Virginia.

On that day, I drove across the Potomac River into the "land of lovers" and purchased lunch in a sit-down restaurant. I was planning to spend several hours there, buoyed by Virginia's recent, notable progress, including electing two Democratic governors and a transgender person to the House of Delegates. But the changes in the state's politics were not all that brought me there. I was making the journey also because of a recently received email from a classmate from St. Agnes School.

☾   ☾   ☾

Just before my twelfth birthday in September 1961, I left my family in Lahore, Pakistan, and flew 7,200 miles as an unaccompanied minor, without an overnight layover, to Washington, DC. I was to enroll as a boarding student at St. Agnes School, an Episcopal school for girls in Alexandria, Virginia. My parents sent me stateside from Lahore alone because they did not want to interrupt my school year. We all believed they would join me in four months.

Greeted and escorted along the way by friendly airline personnel, I hopscotched to Beirut, London, and New York City. From there, I rushed to change airports by helicopter to catch my last flight, finally tumbling into the arms of family friends who were waiting at the airport. Adrenaline had kept me going throughout my voyage and I did not relax until several days after arrival.

Children of British diplomats often made similar journeys, traveling from school in the United Kingdom to their parents' postings and back again. They made these trips several times a year without receiving any special recognition. However, this was not so for the pampered children of US diplomats. In those annals, my trip was highly unusual and I was well aware of its special quality. I was happy to go stateside, because the adventure of making this big trip by airplane on my own thrilled me and I had a strong sense that I was going "home." St. Agnes was located three blocks from our old neighborhood, where my friends Ellie and Bonnie still lived. I imagined I would resume my previous life, including playing kickball after dinner in the street's cul-de-sac.

The previous summer, my father's mentor and boss abruptly left his position as the director of the US Agency for International Development (USAID) for Pakistan. Daddy began serving as acting director and traveled round trip each week from Lahore to Karachi, where the US embassy was located. The Department of State assured Daddy that it would appoint a successor without delay, but that was a false promise.

To my diary, Jane, I wrote on July 29th:

> *I don't like it much in Pakistan. I wish I had my friends like I did on Fontaine St. . . . I am going home in ten days. Yippee!*
> *September 19, 1961–Letter from Jilly today. She is ensconced in St. Agnes School, reports she has 2 roommates & one of the teachers, Miss Stebbins looks "grim." H. had mentioned her, recalling a buxom, determined woman in a girl scout uniform. A letter from Miss McBride [Headmistress] says she looks happy & she & another girl were to have a cake & ice cream for their dual birthdays.* (My mother, Evelyn B. Strachan [EBS], diary)

But the shine of being on my own wore off within one month. On Wednesdays, we invariably ate ham, brussel sprouts, and spoonbread swimming in an unidentifiable, translucent liquid. Everything was wet, including the plate. I missed my parents. I had entered a world of strangers, restrictions, and awful food.

St. Agnes's boarding department, located in a three-story Victorian mansion on campus, held 30 residents. Young faculty members and housemothers occupied several rooms. We ate our unappealing meals together in the dining room and relaxed in the living room, watching televisions shows. We had a Wild West theme going–*Rawhide* and *Bonanza* were two favorites. Boarders also attended a proctored study hall in the school building four nights a week and it was a short walk from the front door. The school offered boarding options because it helped parents such as mine and, likely, because boarders brought in a bit of extra revenue.

I began to write my return address as Misery House, Hardship Lane.

> *October 9, 1961*
> *Dear Family,*
> *I am so unhappy here. Miss Stebbins is making life very hard and I just can't do anything. Please couldn't you write and ask*

Miss McBride if I could have more weekends away? Miss Steb-
bins can be so nice and then she changes and becomes mean. Miss
Webster said that she would speak to Miss McBride and see if we
couldn't have more fun. Mimi Kelly has asked me to come home
with her but I can't. It's just that nobody gives a damn about us
and we're just up there, so what's the difference. ["Up there" refers
to our somewhat isolated dorm room, which was in the rafters of
the boarding department building.] Lisa, my other roommate,
likes school and hates home. I like school too but hate it also. It just
isn't fair. St. Agnes shouldn't have boarding here for us if they
don't care about it. Please mother write and ask Miss McBride
about it and hurry. I know I wanted to come but I don't like school
but I like being here. Love, Jill [written in red ink on St. Agnes
stationery]

School policy allowed full-time boarders limited "away weekends"
and I must have used up all my passes early into the year. Boarding school
was a restricted and restrictive life at twelve.

Mother sprang into action, sending me a letter as quickly as US Embassy mail pouch delivery could manage in 1961.

Lahore–Oct. 13, 1961
Dear Jillybunch:
Mother found your <u>unhappy</u> letter in the ICA box when I
went into the office this morning, and this made mother very sad
too. I showed Heather your letter and am writing to you before
Daddy comes up from Karachi tomorrow.
Now what can you do about a bad situation? Sometimes,
when people are grim and don't smile, it's fun to see if you can get
them to do it. Or, as Mrs. Litsas once said, you smile big enough
for both of you–for you and the one who is grim!
Are your weekends all used up? You see we can only rely on our
friends in the Washington area....
As you know, too, we all get lonesome at times. Heather was

last year and Mother misses Daddy very much when he spends so much time in Karachi. Remember, you were lonely at camp sometimes.

Another thing, if you have time, can you go to ballet on Saturdays? And there's always the family to write a letter to. Or how about some stories? . . .

Anyhow, with all that time on weekends you probably have time to get reading done. St. Agnes must have a wonderful library. . . .

Tonight, Heather and I are going to a Charity Ball Dance although just why I am going to dance without Daddy is more than I know. The Air Force boys will be there, so I shall have to watch them. What a life for an old lady! [She was 54.]

How is T-V? Do they have any good programs? Do you watch it very much?

Do you know this verse?

An epicure, dining at Crewe,
Found quite a large mouse in his stew.
Said the waiter,
'Don't shout and wave it about,
Or the rest will be wanting one too!'
Do your friends know these riddles?

1. *Why is the letter B like fire?*
2. *Why are balloons like beggars?*
3. *What men are most above board?*
4. *What makes the ocean get angry?*
5. *Who sits before the Queen with his hat on?*

Answers: 1. Because it makes oil boil. 2. They have no visible means of support. 3. Chessmen. 4. It has been crossed so often. 5. The Coachman.

Well, my dear, are you practicing up for the Christmas program? Because we shall be there to hear you. We all send you our love,

Mother was a punster but never a teller of jokes or riddles. I realized only recently that she had consulted her friends for the ones she included in her letter. I am not sure how I felt when I received her letter, but now, I love this letter. She was trying to make me feel better. She also offered an important idea for how to deal with troublesome people. I wish I had internalized her advice (and that of Mrs. Litsas) earlier in my life. It might have made me less judgmental of others and less self-absorbed.

From a long distance, Mother marshaled her troops in Alexandria to check on my happiness. This required the expense of international postage for several letters. Her friend Johnnie Walker wrote:

> *This is just a short note to answer some of your worry about Jilly. I am afraid the young lady is the victim of some unfortunatehappens* [sic] *with a little dash of home sickness.*

He reported that another family friend had visited me and found me "well and happy" and "with no signs of distress."
(JW to EBS, October 20 and 21, 1961)

In another letter, December 6, 1961, she offered additional advice.

> *Now, Jilly, don't be afraid to ask questions when you don't understand, or ask the teacher after class. It's no use to learn something you don't understand–otherwise you really haven't learned it, have you? I know it sometimes takes courage, lots of it, to raise your hand when you don't understand, but did you ever think that perhaps there are many others who don't understand either and merely hesitate to ask questions because they think they might show their ignorance. But Daddy and I have always found that it is usually the very wise people who don't mind saying they don't understand but want to try to do so. I think you know by now, too, that while many people may seem gruff, frequently this is just a manner of theirs and they really would like to be helpful. Not everyone has an easy manner.* (I think she was referring to Miss Stebbins.)

Grim Miss Stebbins was my housemother in seventh grade and she scared me because she was strict and unfriendly. I thought her unduly critical of my roommates, Lisa and Mimi. She presented herself as the same grim person when I was a boarder in twelfth grade, although she was not my housemother that year. Her tightly braided bun and her usual posture of her hands across her bosom reinforced her stern countenance. Miss Stebbins lived for decades in the boarding department's turret, which had several floors of its own. We lowly boarding students could only darken its threshold by invitation, knocking gently on the door, of course.

It was more common that Miss Stebbins would appear unannounced in her full-length, flannel nightgown, with her gray hair falling to her knees. This was the worst of all possible encounters. The door to our room was a swingy thing that only covered the middle part of the door frame, like cowboys walking into a bar in a spaghetti Western. She could arrive at any hour, whether we were making, in her opinion, too much noise or simply being quiet and studying late, which she frowned upon. Perhaps she slept in fits and starts, and our unfortunate fate was to disturb her no matter what.

Rules forbade us to leave our rooms after lights out, even to pee. Miss Stebbins shared our bathroom, so each night that we needed to use the bathroom, we risked encountering her on midnight runs.

Initially, we had the bright idea to pee in our cheap, metal trash can. However, this act made a loud noise and required disposal of the night's contents in the toilet the next morning. With this novel use, the trash can rusted quickly and its newly acquired smell gave us away. The house director reprimanded us without figuring out the role that our terror of Miss Stebbins played in our behavior.

Our need to pee, however, did not abate, and we continued our visits to the bathroom most nights. As terrified knuckleheads, we accepted the challenge of being caught yet again. Now we crawled under the door and crept down the corridor through the fire door to heed the call of nature. We reversed the journey to return to the overheated dorm room.

The fire door at the end of the hallway squeaked when opened but we solved that problem by applying oil to the hinges. We thought we were clever by using the oil that lubricated my clarinet keys.

Miss Stebbins might have been grim but we were no angels. I never told Mother about peeing in the trash can and even relating this story as an adult I still carry a modicum of shame in the telling.

Many years later, I found several notes Miss Stebbins wrote to my parents. I had no love for Miss Stebbins so imagine my incredulity when I read: "Jill is a fine little girl and fun to take shopping. I would be so proud to have a daughter like her."

Miss Henricka Stebbins, I never knew ye.

It was Miss Stebbins who accepted the delicate task of explaining to me that my parents were not coming home for Christmas, as they had promised when I left Lahore. I had held on to that promise throughout the fall, but their reason was that their temporary duty had no termination, and they could not leave their posting. It unsettled Mother. At first, she planned to come alone to be with me but that meant separation from Daddy and Heather and there was the expense of the airfare.

My parents asked Aunt Molly, my father's sister who lived in Cleveland, to take me for the holiday and they offered to pay for her babysitting services. Molly was a working woman and she also was a choir director for Sunday church services. Despite unreliable overseas phone or cable service, the arrangements worked out and I had a safe and happy Christmas with Auntie Molly. I forged a special relationship with her that I still carry within me.

Entries in Mother's Diary, December 18, 1961:

> *Keep thinking where I would be if I had followed my go-it-alone itinerary to be with Jill. A letter from Molly said she cried [when told of the newest travel developments] & then went out with Miss Stebbins to choose a peach-colored party dress for the Xmas dance. Our Jilly—it's hard to think of her in such a dress. No word from her since before or after the bad news.*

December 26, 1961:

A letter from Miss Stebbins, house mother at St. Agnes, gave details of vacation plans for our Jill. Poor dear, she will always remember this year, and so shall I. It does seem to me that this illustrates how difficult it is to talk things over properly when the family is so divided.

January 3, 1962:

A letter from Jill dated Dec. 23 sounded like she was going to have a busy time, thanks to Auntie and various of our friends and neighbors even but still she is anxious for us to come & I am egotistical enough to value this.

January 18, 1962:

A wonderful letter from Molly telling about the Xmas holidays. Poor Auntie, shopping, going to Babes in Toyland, helping to write term papers on sons of Virginia, and being suffocated with boasts of the wonders of our family!

I wrote in an undated Christmas card adorned with a drawing of St. Agnes and lamb[1]:

Dear Family, So sorry I haven't written you for so long but I haven't had any stamps. I also have been very busy. How do you like this card? It cost me ten cents. Mother, I am so very, very sorry that you haven't been able to make it for Christmas. You don't know how disappointed I am. I have been counting on it for so long. You were right you shouldn't have sent me to St. Agnes. I am sorry I have cost you so much money. I think I am getting a wonderful experience out of it but I wish I had you. I have sent your Christmas presents and I think they will get their [sic] in time.... Miss Stebbins will presently send you a letter....

---

1 This description was included on the card: "Saint Agnes, a beautiful Roman girl and a Christian, suffered martyrdom under the Emperor Diocletian in the year 304. Because of her youth and purity, the lamb is her symbol."

Mother please write and tell me when you plan to come. I understand about Daddy and Heather and I know I have been selfish.

In my New Year's card, I wrote:

There is a present coming for the family. A present for a real lovely family. A real nice mother, father, sister, and dog. I really miss you all.

I was fortunate to have loving parents and to benefit from relationships they had built with family and friends. These folks looked out for me in my separated year but they could not keep me from feeling lonely. The three-block walk from school to our old neighborhood proved as big a distance as living in Pakistan and relying on letters for communicating with my friends. It had been two years when I returned and many things had changed. Despite Mother's suggestion to walk over to see old friends, it was not possible. The school did not permit solo walks. They required permission slips or a chaperone for every activity.

Bonnie's and our old yard shared a dividing line at the back, which made interaction over the fence natural and frequent. Now, she had new friends and no longer included me. Ellie's mom had committed suicide, and Ellie had moved away with her father, whom she did not like. I worried a little about Ellie's welfare but I spent more time wondering how her mom had hung herself while confined to a wheelchair.

Instead of four months, nine months passed before my parents returned to Washington, DC. Mother described our reunion at the airport:

. . . and there at 1:35 down at the lower doorway stood Jill with a big bouquet of red and white carnations with a couple of chrysanthemums, no taller, looking a little plump, jumping up & down, crying with joy. Was it wonderful to see her!

She offered some observations:

Jill seems to have developed her sense of humor & it was amazing to hear the recording Lew [family friend] had her make of Pakistan, all about the country, its people, resources, our way of living, & the famous trip to Kashmir, when I had a fever of 103 degrees the day before we left. . . . Jill had made me a cake for arrival with 'Hi, Mom' written on it & a card for Mother's Day inscribed with 'Sometimes we fight' then on the next page, the sun coming out of the clouds, 'Fight Ended.' What a girl! (EBS diary, May 12, 1962)

I abandoned my faithful written entries to Jane, my diary, while at St. Agnes, so I have no written record of my parents' long-awaited return. Yet I remember the cake and the Mother's Day card, and I remember being ecstatic to see my parents.

☾   ☾   ☾

In the early 1980s, more than a decade since my last year at St. Agnes, my social life as a Lesbian began to coalesce. When I attended Lesbian dinner parties in Washington, DC., I observed that at many of these events, the hostesses would introduce household dogs before their women guests. This piece of Lesbian etiquette was the butt of jokes that characterized all Lesbians as being socially awkward. Perhaps some of us, including me, were that way, but we also loved our dogs, or doggers, as a friend called them, a linguistic habit I adopted.

On such an occasion, I met a younger graduate from St. Agnes. After we uncovered our scholastic connection, she related story after story about Lesbians at our alma mater. She insisted Lesbians taught us, Lesbians lived in the boarding department, and Lesbian students had crushes on Lesbian teachers.

Her claims bewildered me, as I was living through the initial, awkward phase of coming out. Although my social circle comprised Lesbians and gay men, while I was at work, the closet was my friend. My high school memories were not happy. I had packed them away and was not eager to resurrect them. My new acquaintance's elated recounting was significantly different from the conservative, forbidding institution I remembered. My sister alum persisted in expounding on her version of life at St. Agnes in response to my quiet disbelief. I wracked my memory to recall a single Lesbian inference or anecdote from my high school adventures.

As a teenager, I most likely encountered cultural stereotypes that cast The Lesbian as an independent woman who dressed in a sensible manner from head to toe. But I had neither an awareness of nor language for "unsuitable" relationships, which societal norms tightly concealed and controlled. I could not foresee and had no language for what I was becoming.

That evening, under pressure from my dinner companion, I latched onto my memory of the practical and mysterious Miss Norris as possibly being Lesbian. She taught American history at St. Agnes for 24 years, after serving as a second lieutenant in the US air force. She is buried in Arlington National Cemetery.

Miss Norris's wardrobe included a variety of Scottish, plaid, kilt skirts, with a big safety pin to keep the free side of the skirt in place; that style was *de rigueur* then. In spring, her skirts veered to an A-line, a Ship & Shore collared blouse with a circle pin fastened to it, and a simple, solid-colored cardigan sweater to complete her daily outfit. Her shoes were definitely sensible, probably penny loafers. Pictures in various yearbooks captured her sporty and crisp look that carried a touch of the practical in her ensembles.

Her white hair was remarkable and memorable. It was short, not falling below or over her ears, but curling around them. There was a hint of black underneath, and it maintained its place, never straying into her eyes or onto her cheeks.

Then, another memory--that of Miss Hamilton, the gym teacher and coach--arrived to claim another piece of brain space. My class, the class of 1967, had dedicated our yearbook to her:

> *Through many hours of hard work, Miss Hamilton has devoted herself to improving the athletic standards at St. Agnes. . . . She has made Physical Education a vital part of school life.*

It turned out that 1967 was her last year at St. Agnes after a short tenure of four years.

I had known Miss Norris and Miss Hamilton at the same time but only connected them as faculty members. My informed raconteur breezily asserted there was a relationship between them. "Oh, yes, everyone knew," she said.

I asked my dinner companion if she knew about Miss Norris's puzzling, unexpected death in her early fifties. She had not been ill. I was unprepared for her revelation that Miss Norris's death was suicide. Several years earlier, I had learned of Miss Hamilton's suicide with a shotgun. I wondered if there was a connection between their deaths but knew I would never know the truth.

The closet was functioning effectively when I began to emerge in the late 1970s but its power was diminishing. It made me sad to imagine Miss Norris as isolated and unhappy to such a degree that she took her own life. She had been a positive force in my life as she was for many other girls. Having her as a teacher had been a turning point for my interest in writing and for my self-esteem. She had been an exceptional role model in her forthrightness and self-confidence. Miss Hamilton was a cheerful, friendly presence who greeted everyone . If they were partners, they were definitely in the closet. If, out of necessity, they denied having a relationship, they also concealed their full humanity, which was a profound loss to them, their community, and the school.

As a high school junior, I had heard my classmates talk about the "formidable" Miss Norris. I joined them in revering Miss Norris as a strict, dynamic teacher who exuded a strong, personal reserve. Beside her picture in the 1967 yearbook, a jokester student had offered a humorous and accurate statement of Miss Norris's work ethic, "If you don't work during a vacation, what do you do?" She had high standards. Her American history class was a requirement, which meant that all of us had her as a teacher.

I caught glimpses of Miss Norris through the open door of the faculty lounge or when she was tutoring a group of students in the breezeway that connected the gym to the main classroom building. I think she smoked—a habit that announced independence and freedom for women in the 1960s. Many upper-class students could not wait to have the privilege of smoking in the breezeway.

The differences I had observed in seventh grade were more pronounced when I returned to St. Agnes for my last two years of high school. My peers valued brains but personal appearance, boyfriends, and sports achieved higher rankings. They admired Villager-brand attire and Pappagallo-brand shoes. These popular fashions were an unofficial cultural uniform at a school that did not require uniforms.

My last year, I was a boarding student for the second time and lived in the same room with three roommates. We had a new trash can but the menu had not improved. Themes of loneliness, difference, and anger found expression in my creative writing—some pieces were written for class assignments and others as a replacement for my diary, Jane.

> *I don't really feel a part of anything. None of my friends are happy, and they're only bitter. Just sit around and cut down everyone they can see in front of them along with those that they can't. (JPS essay, circa 1966)*

For a writing class, I submitted an essay on prejudice.

> *One's emotions control one's heart in a manner which is impossible for one's mind to comprehend.... I cite as my example that of prejudice against Negroes. This emotion does not listen to arguments of any sort. It is a blind and stubborn emotion controlled only by one's sentiments. Someone who is prejudiced against Negroes refuses to listen to any reason but what he considers his own. Although the person himself believes he understands his actions, his intellect, if he has any, cannot.* [JPS essay, circa 1966]

Miss Norris handpicked the students for her advanced placement (AP) American history class from the junior class because it was at college level and was graded accordingly. The reading list was challenging and extensive. A key feature of the class was Friday's "Thought Question." Miss

Norris would present a question to be answered within a half hour on one side of a sheet of paper. The lore asserted that if a single word was on a second page, Miss Norris would not read it. There was no point in writing in the margins because she would ignore those markings. Another exercise was to write critical responses to other students' writings.

I wanted Miss Norris to notice me. I was not goo-goo eyed about her but I was in full Notice-Me mode. I wanted the chance to share a conversation with her, or maybe a moment of laughter. She seemed alluring and forbidding, a person of not many words. I cannot imagine how my young self could have sustained a discussion of any length or depth with her unless she had helped me. As an aspiring brainiac, I longed to receive the special, public blessing of being selected for her AP class. I was not self-assured and did not allow myself to think I would receive anointment. But the nod came.

It was thrilling to be in this special, closed society. My destiny did not include conversations with Miss Norris outside the classroom--at least I cannot recall any. In class, I sat with anxiety and heightened anticipation, worrying whether a question would come my way and hoping I would understand the proffered query. The benefits of her tutelage were concrete. I learned good study habits, found a new level of self-acceptance, and learned to think critically about history and other topics.

We also wrote papers on three-hole punch, lined, notebook paper, and I have kept most of mine. Miss Norris wrote her critical notes in the margins, and they are a testament to her rigor as a teacher. She did us the honor of taking us seriously. Miss Norris awarded a "C" for my report on Milton Viorst's *Hostile Allies: FDR and Charles DeGaulle*. She did not think it was much of an analysis: "Your summary is far too short to do Viorst justice!" Critical of my paragraphing, she pointed out my "monotonous sentence structure" and did not spare her signature blue ink in her edits.

In a paper about John Quincy Adams, she complimented the summary as "okay" but asked, "but where is the criticism??" the last word underlined two times. This was another "C" specimen. My summary paragraph continued to take a hit in my analysis of Progressivism . . .

"fine but return to the question! Get to the point!" (again, underlined twice.) Miss Norris did not celebrate the mere recital of facts; she expected the student to employ them to create solid analysis and criticism. My favorite comments, although not when I received them, relate to a report on Samuel Flagg Bemis's *The Diplomacy of the American Revolution*. She noted: "You have the right idea, but several of your points of criticism are either wrong or ill-taken!! (last word underlined two times). She questioned me: "Did you goof off? (I do want an answer to this question, please!) C-." I am sure I never answered her question but I did not goof off. It was more likely that AP history and Miss Norris were light years beyond me. To follow Miss Norris was to learn, which was not an easy path because she did little to make the path softer. You earned your way through. I described her shaping of me for my 50th class reunion memory book: "Many times I have thanked Miss Norris for starting me on the path to thinking more clearly."

I considered myself a B-minus student, and Miss Norris's grading affirmed this self-assessment. In college, I had a steady job writing synopses of wastewater management articles where my hard-won summary skills came in handy. My college roommates pulled all-nighters for term papers but I escaped that agony because I found comfort in writing.

Thank you, Miss Norris.

MARJORIE MAE NORRIS
(1930–1981)

An unexpected email in October 2017 was the impetus for my unusual trip to Virginia in January 2018. It came from a former St. Agnes classmate, Elizabeth. She was the role model for our high school class of 1967, a friend to many, and a steady, pleasant, and thoughtful presence in our class. I never thought Elizabeth would have remembered me, much less reach out to me. Our 50th anniversary graduation celebration was scheduled for October 2017.

*Jill, I'm too lazy to look up the list Alice sent of who is attend-
ing and who's not, but I just wanted to tell you how very much
I'd love to see you there and to meet Jane if she plans to come. I
remember you as a clear-headed, independent thinker and was
so interested in your comments about Ms. Norris and how you felt
she encouraged you to think. What a gift. It's not easy to be an independent thinker at a school like St. Agnes, and I can only imagine it
was hard. I've found, from other reunions, that life has made us all
mellower, kinder, and more open-minded. It would be wonderful if
you can join us. . . . Take care. Elizabeth* (October 8, 2017)

My response took several days to compose. My plans had never included attending my 50ᵗʰ class reunion because of my plentiful negative
feelings about my high school. I had seen none of my former classmates
for 40 years. Yet, Elizabeth's sincerity touched me, and I wanted my reply
to do justice to my emotions from 50 years ago as well as recognize the
unexpected, kind gesture that she had extended to me.

Elizabeth,
*Thank you so much for reaching out to me and for your very
lovely email. I am very touched by your message. You were always
approachable, happy, sincere, receptive, and fun — definitely already a role model even as a teenager!*
*As you obviously gathered, my time at St. Agnes was not with-
out fun and learning, but I also felt very out of place and not able
to be part of the current conversation. I was not always the most
pleasant of people because I was angry. I did feel as if "my way"
was not the norm and was condemned (a strong word, but it feels
right) in some ways. With the wisdom of some living under my
belt, I know now there were other things that contributed to my
not liking being there.*
*Certainly, being a boarder wasn't much fun with Miss Steb-
bins as our house mother (smile). My parents were far away as
well. Although I didn't come out until my mid-twenties, I was*

pretty sure I wasn't going to get married—getting married always seemed to be a big topic with St. Agnes classmates! Of course, as a teenager, I was into myself and so couldn't really imagine that anyone else felt something close to what I felt. Ah, so complicated!

I've never been drawn back to St. Agnes. I still have my Lamb's Tail [the yearbook] which helps me remember the people that I enjoyed. When I received the news of the reunion, I knew I would not go. I'm an introvert and group reunions are not appealing. And now I will be in California on that weekend. All to say, that I won't be here and attending the reunion. You offered the observation from attending other reunions that you thought our classmates were mellower, kinder, and more open-minded. I feel sure that you are right about that. From now on, I will incorporate your observation into how I think of St. Agnes and my classmates—I think I have given no one credit for growing and changing. Elizabeth, I don't know if you ever get to D.C., but if so, maybe we could get together some time. . . . I would like to hear something of your life's journey so far. Again, I so appreciate that you took the time to write to me. Thank you! Have a wonderful time at the reunion. . . . With much respect and gratitude, Jill (October 20, 2017)

Elizabeth arranged a luncheon gathering of five women from the class of 1967, which put me on the road to The Plains on that sunny Friday in January 2018. We had a tasty lunch and a pleasant afternoon. Across a 50-year expanse, my lunch companions looked much the same. I did not have instant recognition, but as we talked and my eyes adjusted to the bright sunlight, I slowly recovered the memory of their facial features and personalities. The general substance of our high school beings was intact, as if dusted off and polished. We (I include myself) were five, decent women who have lived productive lives and were still pursuing interests and causes. I left feeling convinced that besides myself, some of them had voted for Democrats. I do not know what I was expecting, but I bade them farewell with happiness for the unexpected reunion that transpired because of my email exchange with Elizabeth. Our lunch opened an embracing space in my heart for the people who had been my schoolmates and maybe for the grim Miss Stebbins, as well. As Elizabeth wrote:

> *I've found, from other reunions, that life has made us all mellower, kinder, and more open-minded.*

I associate myself with that statement.

☽   ☽   ☽

> *It is almost banal to say, yet it needs to be said: No one ever knows, nor therefore has grounds to judge, what goes on between two people, often not even the people themselves, half-opaque as we are to ourselves. . . . The labels we give to the loves of which we are capable--varied and vigorously transfigured from one kind into another and back again—cannot begin to contain the complexity of feeling that can flow between two hearts and the bodies that contain them.* (Maria Popova, "Brain Pickings," February 24, 2019)

My Senior High School Yearbook Picture 1967

They're all segregationists here [at school]. It's unhealthy to live in a filthy atmosphere like this. It seeps in and makes me squirm. . . . I hate this place and do anything (I mean say) almost anything to shock them. They have no right to their goddamn opinions, because they repeat exactly what their parents feed 'em. (JPS letter to PCB, November 27, 1966)

FOREVER HABEEBEES

1962-1984, 2018

FROM 1962 to 1965 I lived in Cairo, Egypt, with my parents. I was 13 when we moved there, and just a few months shy of my 16th birthday when we left. My father worked at the US Embassy. I attended Cairo American College (CAC) in Maadi, a Cairo suburb where many Americans and international diplomats lived. My parents wanted to live in the city rather than a diplomatic enclave. They rented a spacious apartment on the residential, yet busy, island of Zamalek, which split the Nile River in two parts.

The CAC school bus stopped outside our three-story apartment building that overlooked one part of the river called the "Little Nile." The round-trip bus ride was 30 miles, and it took almost an hour each way because of the heavy traffic of cars, trucks, motorbikes, bicycles, horse-drawn carts, pedestrians in the road, and the occasional camel. The right-of-way belonged to everyone. Wherever my family went, we were the object of stares because of contrasts in how we looked and our obvious wealth. From our blue Rambler, we became accustomed to the crowded streets and the slow pace of traffic, all the while feeling the eyes of the people. When we stopped our car, we would be surrounded immediately by a chorus of requests for *baksheesh* (money).

In accordance with the Muslim week, we went to school Monday through Thursday and a half day on Saturday. CAC offered K--12 classes to international students hailing from 24 countries,[2] housed in a villa that once belonged to Egypt's King Farouk. Egyptian students did not attend CAC because of the differences between American and Egyptian curricula, although we competed in sports. We had American and Egyptian teachers and administrators, and Arabic was an elective. CAC staff included Armenians, British, French, Greeks, and Swedes. Two, white Russians taught French. Their families had come to Cairo after the Russian Civil War (1917--22). As the French might say, our community was *une salade Russe.*

Junior high school was a step up from elementary school. I had a set of friends, and I liked my teachers and classes (except for geometry, which plagued me during 10th grade). Latin and French went well and there were no religious requirements. Extracurricular activities were plentiful, and I had a boyfriend, although that was a secret kept from my parents.

I discovered basketball before I knew there were different rules for boys and girls. In Egypt, girls played boys' rules, which meant that we played full court and could dribble more than three times in a row. I thought that was normal and was surprised and irritated upon returning to the US to discover I was required to play according to girls' rules. That was annoying, while sparking a realization that there were different rules for girls and boys across life.

A few CAC students styled themselves as experts on King Farouk's life, history (both real and imagined), and his notable shenanigans. His full title was "His Majesty Farouk I, by the grace of God, King of Egypt and the Sudan." Our renovated school villa featured a few interesting holdovers from the Farouk era, such as huge, shiny, alabaster bathtubs in the school restrooms. When Gamal Abdel Nasser overthrew the Farouk monarchy and forced the king's abdication in 1952, Egyptians elected him president of Egypt in 1956.

Throughout the school year, including during the colder months when the temperature might settle at 50 degrees Fahrenheit, we CAC students ate lunch outside at picnic tables placed on a concrete slab under a red, canvas awning near the basketball court. We purchased Cokes in small bottles. There was also an Egyptian-manufactured soft drink,

---

2 According to the CAC yearbook, Pharaoh 1963.

which the CAC wags named "Nasser Coke." No student (American or otherwise) was eager to drink it. Its taste was not what we knew as Coke and its origins were questionable. The Nasser government pressured vendors to sell it first, even if they had regular Coke in stock.

The school grounds were dusty (as was most of Egypt) and lovely, tall palms ringed the circular drive outside the official, but unused, entrance. Instead, for some unexplained reason, we entered through the back courtyard, which was closer to the high school building and basketball court. Outside our first-floor French classroom was an Egyptian army encampment complete with camels relaxing between assignments. Their spitting and grunting accompanied our labors in the French language. In spring, the screenless classroom windows were open, and our French teachers developed commendable skills in the use of the fly swatter. They rarely missed but there were a lot of flies. The unanticipated whack of the fly swatter could make a student jump during a hesitant recitation.

Inside the gates of Cairo American College (CAC)

My closest girlfriend was Judy Harrison. Her mother Marjorie taught at the American University in Cairo. They lived near CAC in Maadi, along with David, Judy's younger brother by a year. Judy and I played on the basketball team. She was a year behind me in school but we regularly got together to talk and share the details of our lives. Given the distance between Zamalek and Maadi, we often spent the night at one another's houses. Judy was the shot putter for CAC's women's track team. She was smart, clever, beautiful, and she dated the handsome French guy, Alain Cardon, who was in my class.

One day, when Judy was walking to CAC, a young, Egyptian youth hassled her from his bike, calling to her and trying to stop her in her tracks. She knocked him to the ground with a punch and his bike ended up in the ditch with the front wheel still spinning. Word of her prowess was immediately communicated throughout the CAC community and to the world beyond, for she was never troubled again in her neighborhood.

Mother and Marjorie became friends. Marjorie was the first divorced woman I knew, her status revealed by Mother in a hushed but sympathetic tone. I thought Marjorie was a lot of fun. She introduced me to that heavenly Egyptian sweet halvah, made of ground sesame seeds, which we ate with forks from a round can. Marjorie would burst into Judy's bedroom, scold us for being up late, and then immediately join our discussion no matter the topic, even though she had not been invited. Spending the night in her home was a proven recipe for laughter and discussion and she was more a friend than someone's parent, although I properly called her Mrs. Harrison. In 1973, however, when we were both graduate students at Syracuse University, I called her Marjorie. She died in 1983.

In a letter to Judy, I wrote:

> *Your Mother had many fine qualities--she was brave beyond all measure, appreciative of quality as standard, loving, humorous, engaged, generous, active, interested, and much more besides. Her presence enriched my life. The absence of that presence is already felt and remarked.* (JPS letter to Judy Harrison, April 19, 1983)

David, Judy's brother, died in a hotel in Paris in 1978. By his bed he left a volume of Edna St. Vincent Millay's poetry. He was a gifted sculptor and one of his pieces, carved in white marble and shaped like a toad, still graces my doorstep. Mother purchased it when David was a student. From 1965 to 1983, Judy and I crossed paths many times but I do not know where she is now.

☾   ☾   ☾

I rode the school bus from Zamalek to Maadi with my friends Dee Taylor, Debbie Simon, Russ Dynes, Peter Biella, and Dan Enroth. Peter and Dan hailed from California, which was a mystical place to me. Our bus took a course along the Corniche--a once-elegant avenue by the Nile--after first navigating the traffic crossing the bridge into the older part of the city. Peter lived nearby, and we would talk and wait for the bus on a cold, white, marble bench. In winter, we usually heard the bus before we saw it because of a dense fog off the Little Nile.

With warm weather, the breeze through the bus windows could be lovely, but other times not so much. Sometimes the bus was caught in a traffic jam at a spot in the road where, for a couple of months in the spring, there were tall piles of rotting onions. The stench was disgusting. Our bus had no air conditioning, and we relied on open windows for cool air. The onions appear in my yearbook in a handwritten remembrance from a fellow rider.

> *Haven't you enjoyed those bus rides? But they can't come near the ones this year those lovely onions 'that scent.'*... *Love & Stuff,* *Janie* (September 1963).

The bus was our social platform from which we passed notes back and forth, hinting at crushes and related issues. It did not differ from the usual teenage stew of known and unknown facts about sex and constant speculation about who liked whom.

For my age, my parents gave me considerable latitude to explore the cosmopolitan city of Cairo, population of 600,000 in 1965. They imposed no restrictions on where I could go and set no curfew. I was careful by nature and unwilling to risk parental wrath, which are two qualities that helped me make better choices (or at least better than some of my classmates did). Besides the modern hotels, there were the city's old quarters and the mysterious Muskey bazaar (also known in Arabic as *Khan el-Khalili*), where a plethora of cramped lanes and small shops awaited both the curious visitor and the serious shopper. It was said that a person could find anything in the Muskey.

When with friends, I traveled around the city on public bus but I took taxis for short, solo trips. Engaging a taxi began with securing one in our residential neighborhood and then negotiating the fare before getting in. There were no meters and taxi drivers repeated the claim that they had *mafish fakka*, no change, if the fare was not determined before the ride was completed. In that case, the rider's first choice was to sit in the taxi until the driver produced change while he continued to mutter *mafish fakka*. The second was to wait in the taxi while the driver sought change in a nearby shop or from a passing stranger. Both options required determination.

To board a bus required persistent pushing against the bodies already crammed inside. Egyptian buses allowed little time to hop on or off. Disembarking from a bus involved jumping from the back platform to the street. If the bus was at a standstill it was easy but when the bus was moving, the feat was less gracefully accomplished. I learned after the fact that I needed to keep moving after landing my disembarkation jump.

One night, coming back to Zamalek from Maadi after a dance party, Russ, Peter, and I missed our stop. My companions quickly jumped from the back of the bus but I waited. When I followed their shouted directions to jump, I crashed onto the road. I had several, large bruises to show for my bold hesitation. Although it was difficult to walk afterwards, I hid my discomfort from my parents and my clothing covered my bruises. The parental understanding was that the bus was too dangerous for young women, and I did not want to explain my escapade.

On Thanksgiving Day, November 28, 1964, Americans living in Cairo were devastated when the recently rededicated John F. Kennedy Library of the US Embassy was burned down by several hundred students. Only eight books were salvaged from its important collection of Arabic texts and scholarly books. The response of the Egyptian police and fire departments was completely inadequate, and President Nasser did not apologize, even when the US government threatened to withhold aid. It was not immediately known that the fire was set primarily by Congolese students who were protesting the US role in the Congo.[3]

I remember that night. After saying goodnight to my parents who had briefed me on the situation, I looked out the window of my room. It faced east and I tried to prepare for the sight of rioters coming toward our apartment building. We lived several miles from the US Embassy and were secure, but anything could have occurred. In our previous postings, we had never experienced apprehension on this scale. Cairo did not seem as fun to me after that event.

Mother maintained the household with the help of Fatima, a housekeeper, and various cooks. Fatima was a reservoir of happiness. Her chief duty was the family laundry, which she accomplished with an old washing machine that came with our apartment. Her brawny arms wrangled the clothes with impressive force as she pushed them through the wringer. She finished by twisting the clothes with her hands before hanging them out to dry.

Fatima loved us all. She always greeted me with an enormous hug, and my aloof, teenage self could not convince her to cease and desist. I was her *habibti*, "darling," in the female declension case, as she told me over and over.

Habibi was an often-used Egyptian expression. At CAC, we adopted it as a greeting to our friends. In our usage, we imagined we would forever be *habeebees,* as we called each other.

---

3 For background information, I consulted the archives of Association for Diplomatic Studies and Training (ADST). adst.org.

Fatima getting ready for work

I had a poodle-mix black-and-white dog named Nicky. He was the first family dog for which I had responsibilities, and I loved him. I walked him by the Little Nile on the pleasant, tree-lined walkway that bordered the river. Beyond the wall, I could see the water's edge and mounds of garbage and water rats. Further out, there were beautiful sailboats, called *falukkas*, slipping by. Except for the voices of the crew, they passed silently.

Young Egyptian men attended the technical school near the north point of the island and they walked the same path as Nicky and me. As was the Egyptian custom, they held hands and called to me as I maneuvered by them, trying to keep to the side. Several times, when the sidewalk was less crowded, I encountered a single man masturbating behind a slim tree.

With Nicky, I walked to a nearby kiosk and purchased Egyptian-made bubble gum packaged in gold foil to resemble a coin. From there, I could see into the gated and guarded grounds surrounding the large house that belonged to the revered Egyptian singer and actress Um Kalsoom. Known as the "Voice of Egypt," she was celebrated for her lengthy concerts, which could last several days. Her repertoire included 280 songs. She died in 1975 at 77.

My father was the official liaison from the US Embassy for the US Fulbright Program. Fulbright families, such as those of Russ, Peter, and Dan, were provided modest living stipends and were more likely to live within the city, where rents were cheaper than in surrounding areas. Fulbrighters relied on the local food market, which was limited in its sanitation practices and did not offer American treats such as chocolate chip cookies or its ingredients. Our family had access to a small, US commissary that made American-style cookies easy to make and thus our kitchen was a hangout. My Fulbright friends gobbled them up.

Russ and Peter were Dan's sidekicks in various teenage activities, which I cannot say inspired community spirit. In the Nile Hilton downtown, a metal chain hindered the theft of ashtrays with a heavy, lead ball attached on one end. It was their delight to twirl the chains in the air, the metal ball spinning. The "Enroth gang" stole the chains and left the ashtrays behind. Sometimes I caught murmurs of other happenings, but I never knew those specifics. I learned much later that Peter was ashamed of their disrespectful behavior. He protected me from understanding the full panorama of their tricks, which ensured that I would not tell an adult. Had I known, I would have.

Mrs. Nour was our bus monitor and CAC's history and mathematics teacher for junior high schoolers like us. She was from Pennsylvania, as she constantly reminded us, and she had married an Egyptian. "Nour" means "light" in Arabic. She was bossy and a bit out of her comfort zone, as was I, with cheeky, American boys who paid no attention to her instructions.

Peter and Dan showed her no mercy. They started calling her "Ma Nour" behind her back and then to her face, which required tongue gymnastics to muffle articulation but still get the point across. She identified their disrespect and kicked them both off the bus several times, which meant they had to take public transportation to school but still

arrive punctually, which was not the easiest of tasks to accomplish because it involved an overcrowded bus, a train ride, and a walk.

Judy and I rehashed the antics of the boyish trio at our own unofficial reunion in May 1973. They had left an impression on us. Here is the
summary I provided to Peter:

> *We also discussed our feelings about you, and we agreed that you*
> *were a real trauma to Egypt. Certainly, Ma Nour never got over it.*
> *But I remember being somewhat scared of you because you were so*
> *unlike everyone else who had crossed my horizon. But thank god you*
> *did come across my path sometime. Although I would have to admit*
> *the fact that your James Bondish approach to Egypt was a big part of*
> *my impressions of you.* (JPS letter to PCB, May 23, 1973)

☾   ☾   ☾

Cool Dan of California paid a lot of attention to me, in which I happily and greedily basked. It was a fresh experience to have caught the eye
of a boy. I was an easy mark for him, as he could manipulate my naïve and
conventional ideas. He "introduced" me to surfing, although he was from
Sacramento, which is not known for its beaches. I am not sure he had ever
surfed and I doubt his qualifications as a surfer, to say nothing of his qualifications as an instructor. His main credential was the Beach Boys albums
he had brought with him, and we played them as much as possible. There
was no beach in Cairo but these songs complemented the hot, Egyptian
weather from April to October and the group was American!

> *I get so homesick and all when I hear those old Beach Boys*
> *songs like 'Surfer Girl', etc. I connect Cairo with so many of them I*
> *feel like crying when I hear them. I guess it's just sloppy sentimen-*
> *tality, but it upsets me so.* (JPS letter to PCB, October 3, 1966)

We teenagers experienced American pop culture in a delayed manner, and we had to rely on someone to cough up LP records after a return

trip from the US or the UK. The latest songs could be six months old by the time we heard them. On Thursday and Sunday nights, those in the know listened to an hour-long broadcast of American pop music on Egyptian radio. I became temporarily popular at CAC when Daddy brought me an early album of The Beatles after he stopped in London on a trip back to Cairo. It was the British version, prized, I found out, because it had more cuts than the American LP.

Dan put me down for my adoration of The Beatles and insisted that I listen to the Rolling Stones instead. I found the latter gross, as he knew I would. Their explicit sexual lyrics made me uncomfortable. He ridiculed me for my white, anklet socks and saddle shoes, which, I guess, were not in style. He recommended tennis shoes without socks. Although Mother had signaled her disapproval of wearing tennis shoes off the basketball and tennis courts, I risked her hawk eye and potential ire and tried out Dan's suggested fashion change.

In 1965, mine was a story of teenage heartbreak. The object of my unrequited love was Dan, the one who got away. I wonder now whether his detailed attention to my mostly-selected-by-my-mother-through-the-Spiegel-catalog-wardrobe was a harbinger of his desire to control me. I was crazy about him when we were dating or, more accurately, dating in secret, but Dan was only interested in ratcheting up his conquests. After our first kiss, which was my First Kiss but not his, he spent months flirting with and mocking me, with the mockery being integral to the flirting. Peter tried to warn me but Dan's meted-out attention was flattering and I could think of nothing else. I was both uninformed and unformed.

An important episode in our relationship began when Dan insinuated several times that there was more of his "good stuff" to come my way if I would only utter the words, "California Mountains." His words evoked excitement and confusion. I resisted for many months, which felt like an eternity to my teenaged mind.

In the spring of 1965, Daddy unexpectedly moved to Vietnam per Lyndon Johnson's cabled request. Dependents were not allowed on post, so Mother and I remained in Cairo until the end of the school year, when we would go to the US and wait for Daddy's return. The Fulbrighters were also leaving. These circumstances compelled me to make a date to explore the California Mountains with Dan.

I called him one evening when Mother was at a social engagement until at least 11 pm. Parental rules prohibited me from entertaining boys in the apartment without supervision, so I prepared a lie of omission. I would not mention visits by any boys, and specifically not a visit by Dan, because Mother was not a fan.

But when I heard his voice I lost my courage. Dan knew the purpose of my call but it was not in his character to help me with my predicament; he preferred to savor my twisting in the wind. He insisted I say the sacred words. When I whispered them he was there in astonishing quickness, even considering that we lived only a few blocks apart.

Upon his arrival, Dan and I started to explore California Mountains on the living room carpet. We had scarcely begun our make-out session when Mother's key rattled in the lock. Mother was home much earlier than expected. Abject terror took over.

Dan scuttled up three steps from the sunken living room, through the adjacent dining room, exited the kitchen back door, and down the steps to the street. He left his shoes behind. Mother did not hear him or see his shadow. In retrospect, the interruption was a *good* thing.

She asked me what I was doing. I claimed I was studying on the floor, which was not my usual practice. My clothes were still on my body but I knew Mother would note their rumpled condition. She then asked me about the shoes lying on the carpet. To my eyes, the shoes had grown to an enormous and obvious size. They were dark brown against the light-colored carpet, and I could not conceal the obvious fact that they belonged to a member of the opposite sex.

At that moment I learned that when in a difficult situation, the briefest answer is the best; more so when it is the truth. I said, "Dan's. He forgot them." Without further ado and to my overwhelming surprise, Mother suggested bed was in order since it was a school night.

Flushed, disheveled, and unsure of my footing, I went off to my bedroom, trying to stay in the dark as I navigated the short distance. My heart was still pumping from making out and the unexpected encounter with my mother. I tried to calm down. I felt relieved at escaping her wrath, astonished that she had not said a word about my behavior, and partially triumphant that I had gotten away with breaking the rules. I will never know, of course, but perhaps Mother granted me grace when I least expected such a gift. We never exchanged a word on this topic. Her diary, if she kept one then, is missing.

On the school bus the next day, I slipped Dan his shoes without attracting curious stares or questions. I pitied him for his walk home on the dirty, Cairo streets in his socks. Looking back, it seems more like just desserts.

Dan and I had another rendezvous in Genoa, Italy, that summer. Our families met for a meal before we boarded separate ocean liners home. We found more opportunities to canoodle on the city's streets and staircases, though Mother might have preferred the living room floor for such activity.

I expressed ample angst about our relationship when we returned to the US. From my diary, Easter 1966:

> *Oh, Lord. If I could just explain how I feel. He's just another guy, you say. I don't know. He's lots of things: the first guy who cared about me in any way shape or form, the first guy to kiss me, the first guy to call me "sexy" or even suggest that I might be, but he is not just another guy. He can't be because he is so special. That is the only defense that I have and it's pretty poor. He must mean a lot because I still like him and am not interested in anyone inferior. It's all in my mind. Maybe if I repeat it, I'll believe it. FUNNY.*

Dan was living in Sacramento again, and he had written me a few letters. I was clinging hard to memories of him while processing my feelings with Peter and others by mail.

> *Jill is still stuck on Dan. She must be dumb in the head because she can't realize he's 3,000 miles away and going steady with Debbie or whoever she is.* (Letter from Russ Dynes to PCB, November 4, 1965)

Yet, I was catching on. In a letter to Peter, February 24, 1966:

I got a tape yesterday from Enroth. He always insists that I'm so dumb and helpless that I know absolutely nothing and perhaps he has reason.

In the spring of 1966, Daddy had returned from his Vietnam tour and took a new post in Colombo, Ceylon (now Sri Lanka), as head of The Colombo Plan.[4] Mother and I joined him there in June via the West Coast, Japan, South Korea, and Singapore. While we were in San Francisco, I saw Peter and Dan; I remember the visit with Peter but not with Dan. In October 1966, after I had returned to boarding school, I sent Peter a letter explaining where things stood with Dan:

I was debating the question as to whether I really liked him, or was just thinking about him, because he was all I had. I said that above all, I didn't want him to become a habit and I didn't want to like him, because he held my hand properly. In fact, in light of seeing him again, I couldn't decide at all if I liked him. . . . Of course, when I saw Dan again, I realized my mistake and that I had wasted about nine months in pursuit of quelque chose [something] that was quite unobtainable. It's just that I didn't realize this until I arrived in Ceylon and there was the inevitable 'no mail' waiting for me.

By 17, if my experience with him was any sign, Dan was a versatile player. In his own words:

My love life is OK, I've decided. There is Debby, whom I wrote to all year [while he was in Cairo] but didn't exactly stay faithful to, or really even try. I'm faithful now, but there is another girl who has a part in the play with me, and well, I like night rehearsals. I'm a fool, yes; even in CAC, a small school, the secret

---

4 The Colombo Plan is a regional organization that represents a collective intergovernmental effort to strengthen economic and social development of member countries in the Asia-Pacific region.

leaked out about me & Jill. (Letter from Dan Enroth to Russ Dynes, November 13, 1965)

Dan wrote to me in spring 1968 and divulged he was using heroin. In this last letter, he extolled its wonders and urged me to join him in its pleasures. I did not reply. I tossed this last insult. I can never forget the letter which was long, double-sided, and handwritten in black ink on bright, chartreuse stationery. Long after our teenage, hormonal flicker had faded away, Dan was loathe to stop instructing me in the essence of cool.

For many years, I engaged in a strong, personal deception that Dan died from a heroin overdose. Only recently was I disabused of this notion by Peter Biella.

☾   ☾   ☾

Peter proved to be a cherished confidant and lifelong friend. I preserved an unsorted collection of his letters, notes, and postcards, keeping them in a straw basket for easy transport. His epistles numbered around 50. Peter also kept my letters and they numbered around 80. He photographed my parents' 50th wedding anniversary party and I once hired him to shoot an audiovisual presentation about sanitation in a food processing plant. He is a professor of anthropology at San Francisco State University and an acclaimed filmmaker. Handwritten letters were our chief means of communicating from 1965 to 1975.

> *Ok. There's something that I want to say. Something about your letters, but I can't express it. Sometimes I really feel that I understand you, but at other times not at all. Not that that's a profound statement, but in Cairo, I had you all written off . . . and now I'm finding that there is so much that I missed in you and other people. . . . I'm so glad you managed to tolerate me so we can write each other now, because the correspondence is teaching me a lot. . . . And I thought that it would all end with the eleventh of June '65. Stupid, aren't I?* (JPS letter to PCB, January 19, 1967)

June 11, 1965 is the date Mother and I left Cairo.

There is some quality about you that even to this day still makes you special in my life. It's the same quality which causes you to write a lot of your letter on the back of an envelope in pencil so that it's practically impossible to read what you wrote and practically impossible to get inside the envelope without destroying what you wrote. (JPS letter to PCB, March 2, 1974)

Peter wrote the most interesting details on the back of envelopes. It seemed to be his proclivity. He included drawings and poems, half-finished, just begun, or sometimes completed. It was hard to tell, and it did not matter. He often used capital letters and his spacing was random—his content could reside outside the left column, indented, then not. He used felt pen, pencil, and red pen, which is troublesome to decipher after five decades. He used lots of curious spellings, and logical paragraphing was rare.

Peter typed a letter while in the family car during a severe storm as an experiment of sorts. Another time, a friend typed what he dictated, and I was not sure if I would understand his meaning. The letters reached me in Washington, DC (in care of my parents with a note to them on the envelope); at boarding school in Alexandria, Virginia; at college in Chicago; in Spokane, Washington; at grad school in Syracuse; and in Strasbourg, France. We were young people with plenty to distract us from writing letters, including budding relationships, crushes, dogs (particularly his dog Fido), drugs, parents, politics, the draft, Vietnam, premarital sex, and travel, to name a few urgent topics. Yet, our correspondence, if not regular, was notable for quantity and steadfastness.

Like Dan, Peter questioned my inherited, unexplored conventions but never with cruelty. He was a conundrum wrapped in the male body of an American teenager. Our parents became fast friends and their friendship extended beyond the shared year in Cairo. Peter's older sister Joan was a graduate student at the American University in Cairo and later, we became friends when she worked for the Library of Congress in Washington, DC.

I was 15 (a sophomore) and he 14 (a freshman) but he was years ahead of me in his thinking. I had difficulty appreciating him, so in a gesture of recognition and apology, I wrote:

Actually, though, I could kick myself for not noticing your intelligence, potential, and sensitivity in Cairo. I have a knack for passing over those people who have the most worth. I'm sorry I did that to you. That was an admittance of fact to myself, not an apology to you, I guess. (JPS letter to PCB, June 24, 1967)

A variation on this topic: *I tend to remember more often the gentle side of you–which always seemed to peek around the corner at me at the oddest times. It always surprised me, and I was <u>never</u> once prepared for it.* (JPS letter to PCB, May 23, 1973)

Peter had self-confidence that I lacked and envied. He had already done a lot of thinking about big ideas such as God's existence and the role of parents and teachers. It was important to question their notions and norms, including ideas about the proper length of a boy's hair. He lived as if there were no reward in seeking popularity and he feared nothing, although his actions got him into significant trouble.

Once, Peter joined the three Harrisons and me on a day trip from Cairo to the Red Sea in the Harrisons' VW Beetle. There were no amenities at the beach; no gas stations, no restaurants, no beach chairs, no lifeguards. We brought everything and packed the car to capacity. The calm water was a sparkly, clear aqua and the beach a combination of sand and stones. With no shade it was hot, even in cooler weather. For part of the journey, the road paralleled the Suez Canal along tall sand dunes with the tops of tankers appearing to move through sand.

The five of us started back to Cairo in the late afternoon. In the backseat, Peter, David, and Judy were engaged in lively conversation. Judy, in her exuberance, said "damn" several times. The four of us had heard Mrs. Harrison use this word frequently, but when the word came out of Judy's mouth, Mrs. Harrison chastised her. Silence followed her agitated reprimand. Peter spoke up, "Mrs. Harrison, excuse me, it wasn't Judy who said it, it was me." There could be no mistaking Peter's voice for Judy's, but Mrs. Harrison bought his explanation. She ended up apologizing to Peter for her behavior. He steered the conversation forward and the rest of the trip was smooth as the sea we had just left.

To us, Peter acquired a halo from the trip. Judy and I always laughed at our recollection of that moment while marveling at Peter's successful audacity, for which we were immensely thankful. He had trumped an adult but not in a mean way, and he saved a friend. He had suffered no consequences, either.

Peter inhabited a space that made me judge him annoying and puzzling in his persistence. At the same time, he also pushed the borders of my thinking. For example, if I pronounced a point of view, most likely one that I had heard expressed by my parents, he might offer a question in return that pushed me to clarify my stance. If he pressed his better-prepared argument, my defense was to call him ambiguous. I found him unsettling because he challenged my bonds of conformity and I did not always understand him because he was beyond my experience and capacity.

From the start of our friendship, Peter was a reliable commentator and an unlicensed counselor. He offered me advice that I did not want to accept even though I might have sought his opinion.

I am not impressed because I know Enroth. (PCB letter to JPS, August 27, 1965)

Or he offered observations of my behavior. . .

as I recall, that was the night you said, 'I'm not going to talk about Dan tonight, hear me, Dan?' and other things happened too that I won't bring back to your recall. (PCB letter to JPS, February 11 or 12, 1966)

Funny and empathetic in unusual ways, he looked at the world differently. He was honest. He gave me feedback, assurance, and made me nervous. I worried his storm cloud would sweep me up, for I did not think he was happy. Peter did not respond in the way adults expected, either. He eschewed their approval and voiced no comments that might show he was thinking of reforming. Some adults could have thought he was "acting out" for the sake of it, or that he was "cheeky". My mother thought he needed discipline and she worried he was a dangerous influence on me, her younger, vulnerable daughter. She never forbade me from seeing him but I believe she blamed Peter for my becoming an adolescent, although that was inevitable with or without his assistance. Privately, I admitted he was interesting, but my eyes remained focused on Dan.

Peter supplied a contrast to my self-assessment in a post-Cairo letter.

> *I've been thinking about you since I saw your parents.*
> *It's weird being now much older than in Egypt.*
> *You being a sophomore seemed so remotely older then.*
> *Now I don't think a sophomore so old.*
> *But it seemed sufficient. At the time.*
> *Anyway, you seemed to know what you were doing.*
> (PCB letter to JPS, June 25, 1975)

This undated note written in tiny handwriting on exceedingly small, six-hole-punched notebook paper charmed me. (circa 1970s)

> *Dear Jill,*
> *There are answers to unasked*
> *questions*
> *Within your head*
> *there are answers.*
> *We are part of the answers.*
> *The moon flows*
> *toward dawn*
> *The light of morning*
> *shows us the moon as well.*
> *Let us then be as free*
> *as our energy will let us -*
> *we can create our freedom*
> *as well as our destination*
> *The poem is running out for me.*
> *Life is heavy on my mind.*
> *I wish for my love and a new home outside this city.*

I am anxious about <u>trials</u>.
My mind has been closing for
The last 5 months. Only a few openings have been made. I
must study myself anew. I have never said that about trials before.
It's true. I must never forget my subconscious. I want to be more—
lineward more me-ward
*   Then Society.*
FOR JILL & FOR LATER

He asked me to be his best man at his wedding in 1984, which was an afternoon ceremony in the dining room of the large house he and Amy, his soon-to-be-wife. shared with several others in Philadelphia. The house had once belonged to a diva opera star, and the attic contained cast-off, glorious costumes. He alleged that I was better dressed than him, and I was. I wore a beautiful, dark blue, smoking jacket that I purchased at a second-hand shop for $5.00. The jacket's lapels had a shiny tinge, and I wore a white tux shirt and matching pink bow tie and cummerbund. Oh, and handsome, black dress pants. After the festivities, I drove back to DC and arrived in time to sing in a concert of the Lesbian & Gay Chorus of Washington, DC.

A September 22, 2018, email from Peter illustrated he had not lost the artistry of his communication:

The numbers are right and Wednesday is reserved. Letters ahoy
With love P

I had no trouble understanding that four of us would meet for lunch on Wednesday, September 26th, and that he knew I would bring his old letters.

☾   ☾   ☾

So, I wrote back my letter saying how much was going on and
still there was life and breath and still, jill, there was life—and
your second letter told me about the jefferson airplane being there.

I am a real egoist to presume that what I want you to talk about is really what is worth talking about. I guess I am limiting what I want to hear. BUT NOT REALLY. I just want life in your letters. I really felt pain in the letter I just read from you, but I also felt you—and remembered what you were like after a long time of not remembering. (PCB letter to JPS, circa spring 1970)

But I think I have overcome my self-doubt to a large extent. . . . Please don't worry about me. I am, in fact, very happy. Many things are working out well for me. My parents and I are trying to enjoy each other as people for the first time, my research is going well for my paper, and I am full of energy to do many things with myself and for other people. In toto, I am in good shape, not at all oppressed even though I am the child of an upper middle-class couple. Just remember, you can't always get what you want. (JPS letter to PCB, December 1970)

Self-portrait, Peter Biella, c. 1973

PETE AND ME

1971–1987, 2019

ON JANUARY 14, 1987, in a funeral home on the west side of Chicago, I said a goodbye to a friend who had died three days earlier. His name was Peter J. Meehan[5], most often called Pete. I had expected to know him all my life. We met through music and laughter, singing in Blackfriars, a University of Chicago musical theater group. He was a sweet, Polish-Irish, Catholic, gay man who emerged from a closeted life. He and I were friends, then briefly lovers, and finally something beyond either category. He never fully disclosed himself to me.

We were close, capable of being silent together. We might lie together at night, stroking the other in the most soothing way. We fit together, fulfilling no conventional understanding of male/female relationship. We took our comfort where and when we found it, not always understanding its source or our own needs. Pete and I had a joking pledge that when we were in our mid-forties, if neither had found a partner, we would marry each other. He never made it to 40, much less 45.

---

5 Pete's funeral card provides the initial "J." Elsewhere, I recorded his name as Peter James John Meehan. That might have been a joke.

We discussed these feelings a few times face-to-face but, as young intro-verts, intimate conversation was difficult, and we were inexperienced at ex-pressing emotions aloud. Instead, what we wrote–Pete in his letters to me and me in my journal—-revealed the depth of our feelings. Thinking alterna-tively brought confusion and distress. We had little hope of acceptance from friends and family, while at the same time questioning our own ideas and emotions. What words were available to describe what we meant and could mean to each other? Could we possibly create a lasting relationship?

In a letter to Peter Biella, my confidant from high school, I sought advice. This Peter grew up in California and he had been a receptive, thoughtful listener. It was easy to tell him about my feelings. He re-sponded to my tale with this:

> *I more or less subscribe to the religion, 'Try to avoid mind-fucks.' Pete sounds like an attractive, warm, and sympathetic to-tal mind-fuck.* (Letter from PCB to JPS, c. 1972–73)

Diagnosed with pneumocystis before anyone inside or outside the medical profession knew much about AIDS, Pete told his parents in one labored breath that he was gay, and in the next, that he was dying. A social worker stood in his hospital room to assist in his telling. This was the same hospital room in Chicago where nurses and technicians wore yellow rubber gloves and left his food outside the door out of fear of him and his disease.

In December 1985, I made a day visit to Chicago from Washington, DC, where I lived. Lying in a hospital bed, Pete looked awful, his tiny frame significantly diminished, and his sweet skin taken over by huge, purple Kaposi Sarcoma (KS) splotches and tumors that turned his hand-some looks grotesque. His appearance alarmed me and tugged at my na-ivete, which was shaded by a bit of a Florence Nightingale complex that made me think my visit would be significant and helpful.

I am ashamed even now to write that I could not overcome my repul-sion to this physically altered, strange-looking man who had always been at-tractive to me. I only managed to touch him in a distanced way by rubbing his feet as I stood at the end of his bed. He smiled at me through his weakness and the phenobarbital-induced haze. Several months later, he wrote:

> *I think I never did let you know how much I appreciat-ed your visit while I was in the hospital.* (PJM letter to JPS, March 6, 1986)

Pete's aspect, however strange and shocking to me at first, would become depressingly recognizable over the next decade as other friends became ill. His last year was terrible–there were few community services for AIDS patients–and he was alone most of the time.

At his Catholic funeral with open casket, the priest made no mention of Pete's young age nor of AIDS. Without access to the backstory, the uninformed attendee would not have understood what had happened to Pete, who died a month shy of his 39th birthday, and, if our pact had held true, about six years shy of our marriage. Instead, somehow I was a pall bearer which was a huge departure from our whimsical, half-serious plans and from Catholicism's norms.

The dark, maroon-colored signs of his KS tumors had been erased from his face. I understood for the first time that people may ask for an open casket to forget the visual ravages of disease on loved ones. I was outraged and furious that the Catholic Church would resolutely and dutifully remember Pete (and others like him) without mentioning his youth and what had taken him away. A conspiracy of silence, propagated by family, mortician, priest, and even me, reigned over Pete's death.

I have rarely found peace in what is said on these occasions. On that terrible day, my upbringing helped me to behave but my silence covered my stoked anger.

> *Do not go gentle into that good night,*
> *Old age should burn and rage at close of day;*
> *Rage, rage against the dying of the light.*
> (Dylan Thomas, 1914–1953)

I would sing and hear these words many times in the next five years. They are a license for anger, and anger is necessary for change. Pete's birthday was February 26th. He was a half year older than me and he has been dead now for over three decades.

(((

Pete and I were cast in "The Democratic Way," a student-written-and-produced musical that opened on the stage of the University's Mandel Hall on April 30, 1971.[6] We knew each other in passing in our student apartment building but the play was our first encounter outside those walls. He enjoyed acting but could not sing. He was a wonderful dancer. I could sort of do all three.

When I read through Pete's letters 33 years after his death, I welcomed the rediscovery of his wittiness and humor. I had retained a general memory of his self-deprecation and depression–he was rarely satisfied with his life. So, it was a gift and a surprise to be reminded of his easy, supple cleverness and his friendly, loving personality.

> *Lots of people have been by the store lately, shopping for gifts before Christmas mostly. I suppose I should be specific and list a whole bunch of names of people who ask me if I've heard from you or of you. But I won't. They were just being polite I think. But, anyway, from all their empty little hearts 'Merry Christmas.' I think I've grown cynical in my old age.* (PJM letter to JPS, Fall 1974)

He was a keen follower of local and national politics and his letters, which contained tiny drawings and poems, captured his concern about Vietnam, elections, and discrimination. He cursed Nixon, of course.

In a letter to me dated February 1, 1973, Pete wrote:

---

6 The script was written by Marc Primack and Mike Dorf and featured songs from several composers. The RAP wrote: "The show is a light-hearted story about the 'making of a Presidential candidate.'" (April 29, 1971, Vol. 1, No. 11). Primack and Dorf were ahead of their time in their understanding of presidential politics.

Tomorrow completes the first week of peace and yet my world seems unremarkably the same. I do not feel more peaceful. Neither do the people I see appear more peaceful. Maybe the fighting in Asia has stopped, but the unrest in Chicago continues. Nixon has said that those that deserted America in her hour of need will not receive amnesty. For that I hate him. He has said that the people who are at least happy with the ceasefire are the ones who wanted peace at any price. For that I despise him.

Once, he invited me to a Friday night folk dancing group in a parking lot. Bundled up against the Chicago cold, we soon warmed up. LP records spun on a record player connected by a long chain of extension cords running into a nearby building. The music and dancing halted only when there were no more requests from those gathered. I did not know any of the dances, but Pete was a divine partner and leader; he easily swung me around, which made me feel marginally graceful. Pete was naturally well-acquainted with the polka, but he confessed in my ear after two or three dances that he was making up the steps to everything else. He was a clever improvisor and confident in his ability to be "close enough" in his choice of steps to blend into the crowd. When I was lonely and living in Syracuse, he suggested a folk dancing group as a remedy.

Syracuse must have one somewhere. That way you can get some exercise and meet people like George & Diane & myself. Only the best people folk dance. (PJM letter to JPS, January 13, 1973)

Pete's family lived on Chicago's west side, five miles from the University of Chicago campus on the south. Five miles was far for a student living in a cocoon on campus but close enough for me to join his family for Thanksgiving at his grandmother's apartment. The next time I would travel to this part of the city would be for his funeral.

For Thanksgiving, a long line of mismatched tables took up almost all the space in the combined living and dining rooms. His grandmother immediately gave me a nickname when she greeted me by saying, "Hello, Bright Eyes." Perhaps, she could not remember my name, but whatever the case, I felt special to be recognized so readily.

After the traditional feast, the men gathered around the TV while the women went into the kitchen to clean up. Pete joined the women. Pete had not told his family his secret and I did not know it then, either. I was in love with him and happy to be with him in any capacity. He was sweet, silent, mysterious, and strangely spontaneous. Pete's family was both a boon and a burden to him. As his siblings married and propagated, the pressure to conform haunted him.

> *My parents are coming North [from Georgia where they had moved] next month for a combination of things a) the wedding of one of my cousins b) their anniversary c) the anniversary (50ᵗʰ) of one of my great aunts. It will be nice to see them again. ... I think my family is the antidote for most of the things that bother me (except, perhaps, my family).* (PJM letter to JPS, Fall 1977)

The summer following our Thanksgiving with his family, he borrowed his brother's truck, and we made a day trip to the 4ᵗʰ of July parade in Milwaukee to see the Clydesdales. It was crazy hot and there was no AC in the truck, so we drove with the windows down, radio volume high. It was thrilling to be with him. I remember he enthusiastically sang along (although he was not a singer, as already noted) to "Take it Easy" by the Eagles[7] which was popular that summer. I had heard the song but it took on new meaning on that drive. Pete knew all the lyrics. I could tell that he identified with the man's stress expressed in the song but I had to wonder: Was I a controlling woman or one who wanted to befriend him? Both could have been true. Wrapped in his secrets, Pete provided no illumination.

---

7 "Take it Easy," released by the Eagles in 1972.

In January 1972, I wrote to myself:

Mr. Meehan is immediately identifiable . . . by his pointy head, wire-rimmed glasses, his handsome mustache, his innate dedication to evasiveness, and his occasional gestures of pure sweetness. . . . [He has] a slight inclination to a wicked twinkle in his eye at unexpected moments.

Peter J. Meehan, c. mid-1970s

Pete graduated in 1970 and remained in Chicago working at the University bookstore. This was a job that he did not like, or about which he shared ample complaints. Although he left the bookstore for employment at University of Chicago Press, he never found much pleasure in his professional work, which lasted 14 years.

I left Chicago in fall 1972, at first to work on my brother-in-law's congressional campaign in Spokane, Washington, and then to enroll for further graduate study at Syracuse University in January 1973. It was not easy for me to leave as I loved the university and my life there. I returned to Chicago and to Pete as frequently as time and my graduate student budget would allow.

My journal does not record the moment when Pete told me he was different, but it was in early December 1972 when I passed through Chicago from the West Coast on my way to my parents' house in Washington, DC. As I had done many times before, I told my story to my confidant in a letter.

> *Being in Chicago was good and sad, alternately and together. I stayed with Pete which was good. I don't really think I would have seen very much of him otherwise, and I do go to Chicago to see him. We were closer and more comfortable with each other and it made me happy to come home to him at night and to awaken in the morning next to him. But he and I have a most peculiar (that is actually Pete's word for it, <u>je crois</u>, for lack of any other word) relationship. At the end of <u>Justine</u>[8], Lawrence says, 'Does not everything depend on our interpretation of the silence around us?' and this is how I view my being with Pete. All our really good communication is silent and understood and it is a new and difficult experience for old verbose Jill, who finds talking second nature to her.*
>
> *So one night after lying in silence, Pete said to me, 'I am an attractive, warm, and sympathetic bisexual who doesn't feel particularly heterosexual at the moment.' His voice took on an incredible steel quality that I recognized from past dealings with him as meaning that it was hard for him to say that. I said, 'Okay, Pete,' and he clung to me tightly, so tightly.... I've never had to deal with anything like this before, and as you might imagine or predict, his one-sentence statement confused me. So most of my 2 1/2 weeks in Chicago were spent telling Pete silently and carefully that I still loved him and that I could accept him any way that he was. So, our relationship was better, and in some ways more dear. I really have a limited concept of what it means to be bisexual, and at first, I wasn't sure I could handle it.... For my own well-being, a certain self-imposed removal from Pete might not be a bad idea (and distance does that to a certain extent anyway) but simultaneously, I don't want to hurt Pete, and I am heavily involved in all this. His silence and the break of the silence told me that.*

---

8 Lawrence Durrell

When I was packing to leave, I forgot a dress in the closet and Pete found it. He said, 'It's a good thing I found it, because I would have had to tell my parents the truth if they found it.' 'What would you have told them?' I asked. 'That I was a transvestite.' I said, 'Well, then the real truth might be a little easier for them to accept.' And I rushed to Pete and hugged him with many 'sorrys' superimposed. Pete said, 'Hey, that wasn't nasty, it was funny. I thought the same thing myself.' And that incident made me smile for a long time, because Pete can more easily accept himself than I can accept him, or my own self for that matter. (JPS letter to PCB, December 9, 1972)

Both Pete and I had an extended and understandable period when we denied reality, which became more complicated because we were not denying the same reality. Pete was struggling with being gay (although he had first named himself bisexual), and I was struggling with loving Pete who was gay. I counseled myself:

The only thing you can be and do is to be a warm sympathetic friend who gives but doesn't take. . . . I just want to comfort you and tell you it's okay, okay to be what you have to be--okay to be Pete. Okay to touch me. Last night, lying with you, you snuggled up to my shoulder, and my hand on your ass--I felt your strength, peace, and unrest. Pete, I wish I could help, but all I've got is my own problems and hang ups and the money to buy rum sometimes. I can't even conceive of what it means or what I've done to you with insensitivity and carelessness. (From an undated sheet of paper in my handwriting)

Despite Pete's declaration, I remained confused and so did he. It was Pete who took the leap and clarified his feelings in a letter dated March 21, 1973. I had visited him during my spring break from Syracuse and afterwards he sent this letter.

I've been trying to think of some way around this--thinking that if I can avoid it long enough you'll forget about it and I'll forget about it. But you won't and I won't. We both know. So here goes.

Dear Jill,

I can't let you come to me anymore. The strain is too much for both of us. You get frustrated and scrawl 'I need an outlet for my love' on the newspaper. I read it and other things--like your mind and your heart--and know that feelings like that shouldn't happen to anyone. And I feel guilty for letting them happen. You feel bad and I feel bad and I can't bear it anymore.

So I write to you and you write to me and we both speak to and are silent with the other. There is nothing mysterious there. We are--what? Less than lovers, more than friends? Friends at least. We'll see each other and not be shut out of the other's life, but not shut out of our own either. I can't say any more right now.

Love

Pete

That's the letter. I started it Wednesday when you were reading in the bed and before Paul [mutual friend] got here. I threw the original away when Paul got here because it was such a crappy feeling to write something like that and I couldn't and did not want to concentrate on it and he was a good excuse to chuck the whole thing. About that same time I found a poem. I thought you'd appreciate it but I didn't show it to you, because.

ACROSS THE TABLE AT BREAKFAST

You join me half-awake, half-sleeping,
settling down to the chair as if into bed.
The affection of your dreams for you last night,
which has smoothed your face, drains fast
through my clang of dishes, the gurgle of
coffee. Soon, half-full of breakfast,

you will utter your first unchosen words.
They will come between us like children,
hands in their pockets, with nothing else
to do. And then they will take sides.
—*Greg Kuzma*[9]

It could be worse. It will be better.
Peter

He drew a small flower next to his name.

In my journal entry on March 24, 1973, I copied the Kuzma poem and Pete's words: "It could be worse. It will be better."

His sexual preference (his word at the time) was shocking and over-whelming. I did not know any gay people, or at least I thought I didn't. I had wondered about Pete ever so briefly when I encountered him on a spring night in 1971 as he emerged from a group of people who were coming from a gay protest on campus. His sudden appearance seemed a bit odd but I did not think about it at the time because I was happy to see him. After his revelation to me, I remembered this incident and I realized that when he saw me, he separated himself from the group to protect his secret. This realization served as a testament for me on the confines of the closet.

Through a process of mutual, see-saw persistence that did not necessarily include mutual understanding, we grew closer, although we were not always happy with each other. Our closeness happened despite anger, pain, and confusion on both our parts. We wanted to be connected, and we had to figure out how to do that. We knew no models for what we wanted to be.

Pete became my resource for all things gay. It turned out that I had a lot of questions. In response to one query, he wrote:

I wouldn't worry too much about Kathy's [a Lesbian room-
mate in Syracuse] remark about some women preferring to be

---

9 Greg Kuzma, b. 1944, published more than 300 poems in the 1970s in prestigious journals. Wikipedia. Strange connection, he received his BA and MA from Syracuse University, which I did not know until I looked him up for this footnote.

with gay men[10] as being a sign that you necessarily have to fear only being with and liking gay men. I have heard similar statements before and have usually reacted negatively to them. I think that it is safe to say that most people in the world, both gay and straight, prefer to be with people who do not intimidate them. Why would anyone like to be with someone who makes one feel less than human? I am not sure but I think that this is one of women's liberation's points.... That both men and women are people and that each should be treated as a human by the other and by others of the same sex. I really cannot speak from a platform of experience in this matter. My orientation is not with the gay subculture. I don't patronize gay bars. I don't 'cruise' to see what I can pick up. I don't really care to be part of that world either. My brief excursion into it made me convinced that the whole thing is pretty sordid and dehumanizing. (Maybe I'll tell you about it later.) (Letter from PJM to JPS, April 12, 1973)

Pete was still struggling and wrestling with coming out in 1973--74 while I was studying in Strasbourg, France. He described his emotional turmoil.

All these feelings go right into and come right out of some very old fears/places inside of me. There has always been a place inside of me which says that I will fail when something becomes important to me. This fear also applies to the importance of people in my life. Co-existent with this fear is that in my failing, pain to both myself and to others will be inflicted. So far both fears have reasserted themselves with a great deal of accuracy. I think however that I can face up to these fears and dispel them, by changing myself. Hopefully the changes that I make will be for the better. I am already aware of some shifts in my attitudes.... I think that I have achieved mental and emotional adulthood. My idea of myself has changed so that I do not view myself as an eternal

---

10 These women were called "fag hags" by some, not a pleasing appellation.

seventeen, but now see myself as a more accurate twenty-six years of age. . . . Also, I no longer feel as depressed as I have for the last three months. . . . This has really been self-indulgent of me. And this is only in response to the first three or four lines of your letter. (PJM letter to JPS, November 30, 1973)

Living in Strasbourg, separated from kith and kin, brought a period of self-contemplation and reading outside of my regular academic studies. I began to relish the independence of being a single woman living far from home. I was learning about Feminism.

I still worried about Pete.

He has never taken so long to answer a letter. Sometimes I wonder how soon he will commit suicide. Isn't that horrible? I just have a pit in my stomach about him and all my reasoning with my mind doesn't erase it. (JPS letter to close friend BH, January 29, 1974)

While I was in Strasbourg, Pete moved into a new apartment. He was slow to unpack and set up housekeeping. He wrote:

In response to your inquiry--No, I have not yet had my gas turned on. For one thing I have only been in this apartment for two months and I see no reason to rush into anything. Secondly, there is an energy crisis in this country and I am doing my part to help conserve fuel. Thirdly, I have been too busy and have not had a chance to stay home and wait for the gasman to show up. (PJM letter to JPS, October 29, 1973)

I received this news with laughter—accurately or not, I thought of it as tongue-in-cheek and pure-Pete humor. Not once did I consider it might reflect depression. I don't think he ever considered therapy, which, in those days, was a radical step and an expensive proposition.

From Strasbourg, I strongly suggested that Pete come for an extended visit. I thought a change of scene would do him good and give us a chance to work out the shape of our relationship-friendship and maybe come to an agreement on a name for whatever it was we were doing with each other.

> *Speaking of the affairs of the heart . . . remember when I predicted that Pete was about ready to ask me to marry him? When I got back yesterday, there was a letter from Pete after nearly 3 months of silence. The letter was short and desperate and hinted that my last letter (which reasoned carefully through his and my relationship and explained why I had to remove myself from him, etc.) was a blow, because he had hoped that my feelings would have remained the same through all this time. . . . When I think I've conquered my confusion, I am suddenly touched by him again. And he obviously feels it too. Well, I refuse to waste any more time on paper on this topic at the moment, but I thought you'd be interested.* (JPS letter to BH, February 24, 1974)

I then wrote:

> *After some debate, I wrote him today and told him to quit his job and come and stay with me for a while. I'm sure he won't do it, but at the same time I feel I should throw out every lifeline that I can to him. In this letter, he talks about his shame for himself and his life, and I can't help being slightly melodramatic about him and wondering just how far his desperation will carry him. Maybe it's silly on my part but I do worry about him. Maybe it's no solution for him to be with me, but I think he has to get away to where no one knows him and he can begin to put his pieces back together again. But at the same time he needs someone else close to him to be nearby. I just don't know, but I can't really help him.*

A few days following, I recorded:

A letter from Pete informs he is coming, and I am pleased! I'm sure that he made the decision on his own before receiving my two express letters which makes his decision to come of an even-freer quality. Somehow I can't help feeling that his coming and our being together will finally provide some absolute resolution of our relationship, and I must admit that the anticipation of such a situation of 'resolution' is terrifying to me. If he were to ask me to 'marry' him, I just don't know what I'd do or how I'd react. Logically I know there would only be one response, i.e., a negative one, but emotionally I am still much entangled with him without any clear insights about my involvement with him.[11] (JPS journal, March 7, 1974)

My Strasbourg apartment barely qualified as a studio. I shared my Murphy double bed with solo visitors, and a second guest could sleep on an additional hard mattress that doubled as a couch. Pete stayed for two weeks. Part of his visit was shared by a boyfriend, or potential boyfriend; I was never to know which. It was difficult to ask these questions. Pete and I had a couple of days alone in which to reconnect, which we managed without too many hassles.

My journal chronicles his visit.

Well, it seems that 'resolution' may be imminent. But who can tell? . . . Pete arrived on Friday night and I've been more or less impressed by my rather--so what?--reaction. . . . His whole attitude towards life, etc. is self-centered, an unfortunate quality to my feeling at this moment. Oh I can feel the pathos in his life, but I no longer want to touch it. And therefore when I realize that he is telling me little of his life, I find myself uninterested and curious alternately. I can't decide what my role should be--ever consistent friend who asks no questions or a gentle prodder? And yet he gives me no clues. However, the resolution of my feelings is

---

11 I might have been nurturing my Feminism but on the topic of marriage, I held the conventional point of view that the man had to ask.

finally apparent to me. . . . The world is outside my window and I believe I could change it someday. Perhaps when my courage begins to match my ambition. (JPS journal, April 16, 1974)

On April 27ᵗʰ, I wrote:

Since his arrival, he has relaxed a lot and obviously the time alone without emotional pressures (not even from me this time) has helped him. But I fear his European trip may be a brief respite only in the tragedy of his life. He intends to return to the bookstore.[12] . . . Sometimes when I see middle-aged gay men at concerts, I can see Pete being the same way--a lonely 45 with no one to seek out. And in a way he creates the situation for himself. His paranoia and secretiveness make it impossible to ever really touch him. That's another chapter ended. (JPS journal, April 27, 1974)

After Pete's Strasbourg visit, we continued to send letters, although not as frequently, and I devoted much less time in my journal dissecting our relationship. I spent July and August 1974 working in Chicago before returning to Syracuse to continue my PhD studies. It was the summer of the Watergate hearings and at my job, coding college applications, we listened to the hearings on the radio. They were top of mind for everyone I knew. Pete and I socialized that summer, gingerly--we weren't sure what to expect of the other. By then, we were unequivocally dating other people. We did not know our relationship was going to face a twist unlike any we had experienced together up to that point.

Upon returning to Syracuse in the fall of 1974, I fell in love with a woman. I told Pete on the phone and recorded his immediate reaction:

He was quite ecstatic, quite fantastic and asked, 'Does she laugh?' Something makes me think he may begin to talk to me. (JPS journal, December 6, 1974)

---

12 That is, employment at the University of Chicago bookstore from which he had taken a leave of absence for his trip.

A letter dated January 2, 1975, arrived.

Please don't think that long silence has meant that I haven't been thinking about you. That's not true. I have been
A lot.
But I don't know what.
You've confused me. As much as I've confused you you've confused me. As much as I've confused me. Jill?
It's just that the thought of you with Lynne is strange to me. Not repugnant. Not catastrophic, just strange. It's outside my realm of experience and therefore something I can only get used to, not something I can know.
I wrote some things down that night after we had talked on the phone. They will be in this envelope too somewhere. They're real feelings. They are the poem I've always wanted to write for you but not 'THE POEM' I've always wanted to write for you. That, I guess is still inside me somewhere with all those other feelings I've got from/for you. . . .
Are you ok? Which is another way of saying, of asking How are you? (I don't mean just physically but in your Self, in your 'kimuch.')
Are you centered? Got your yin & yang all balanced? These questions to the woman of whose child I should have liked to have been the father. (The phone just rang & I half expected it to be you but I also 'know' you won't call 'til I get in touch first. That's fair. That's the only thing to do.)
I think I have the fear that I shall be put out of your life. That's a pretty big fear in me I guess. Sort of smacks of instant oblivion or something. Delayed death, maybe? I don't know. There's a lot I don't know. . . . (PJM letter to JPS, January 2, 1975)

If I wrote in response to his letter, I have no record. I remember his letter arrived after his silence. Although my life and journal reflected my new romantic interest in Lynne, I took time to vent about Pete's letter.

What pissed me off about Pete's letter . . . that he would be so conventional as to refer to me as the mother of whose child he wanted to be the father of . . . he puts me in a slot of motherhood and respectability also. I was his path to status and acceptance. I understand, Pete, but I resent. The inadequacy of words? He writes that my being with a woman confuses him, it seems strange, and I invite him to say whatever he wants or feels. Yet he <u>never</u> gave me that option, just banged me over the head late one night/ early one morning and I was expected to find it somewhere in me to understand and accept within me never with his help. Gee, I'm sorry, Pete. Just buckle up and bite your lip. Accept it if you will, it makes no difference to me. I don't know whether I in fact really feel the hard way I am writing but I definitely need to write the hardness down. You write that it is not within your experience—is lesbianism so different? What the hell do you mean? I know you are struggling with your words. . . .

Pete, why write me now of death and oblivion when I cannot help and do not want to? Why do you insist upon clinging (no, it's not that, <u>it's just expressing</u>) after I have left for good? I left months ago. You made no sign except to show me the door for which I hindsightedly thank you, but I left as my decision as my growing and you gave no reassurance. Goddamn you, you presume to pull me when you no longer may, when I no longer want it. Haven't you learned yet that you can't play with people like that? Don't send me expensive books and don't try this again.
(JPS journal, January 14, 1975)

Following another phone call about two months later, I started to forgive him.

Almost 1am is not the time to begin about Pete and yet I push on. He worked himself back into my consciousness easily; there was the same hesitance, the same reluctance to communicate, and unfortunately the same ease of friendship for me. He's like an old, comfortable slipper, hard to throw out. And, I do care, there's

nothing the matter with that. I care, he cares, the feelings are com-
fortable, old friends are something I have little of. Yet the same
old thing, the same dissatisfactions, the same despair. . . . What
can one hope for? . . . I want to help and yet do not want to yet
know there is no use—PJM to be a suicide statistic one day? . . . I
fantasize on Pete and me together in old age, tied by bonds which
no one understands not even us, waiting for death to set us free. I
discard this. In my future, I see no such fantasy as reality, but for
that one instant I am chilled. He tries to explain his letter—there
were many ways to understand it, yet I still see only one, the way I,
and later Lynne, understood it. I explain about being pissed, but
that instead of shutting him out of my life I opened my life to him,
because my friendship to him with him is important. I am not
impressed that he has been calling for 3 days, that he memorized
my phone number, that he is calling me long distance—before his
tossing of this doggie bone would have been sufficient to keep me
speculating for hours on the precise meaning of this and that. But
tonight I only noted them after hanging up, and I hung up first,
saying that my beer was waiting. My life is here, Pete. And no
longer in Chi-town. And I am impressed I hung up first. I have
come along way out of the PJM depths to this point. (JPS journal,
March 19, 1975)

After I moved to DC in 1977, Pete visited me several times (sometimes with a boyfriend—there were several). I went to Chicago as I was
able. We corresponded and talked on the phone. Always, we had fun
when we were together. We had grown in our understanding of each
other and could enjoy our remarkable friendship.

Pete is coming to visit [to my parents' house in DC] and John
[his boyfriend] too. I gather that this is significant, John approves
of me, likes me. I feel odd about it in some ways—am I never to
see Pete alone again? . . . I just find it odd that John wants to come.
But perhaps he's not the one to feel these kinds of tensions. (JPS
journal, May 17, 1976)

Driving back from Mt. Vernon yesterday, suddenly I remember what it was like to love Pete, to lie with him. The intensity is a little too much. . . . Strange—I haven't thought of Pete's sexuality in a long time nor of touching him. . . . Pete has grown up and I am so happy for him, he has needed this for so long and for such a loving person he should have the best. I felt my good-bye tears coming and left. When will I stop crying when I say good-bye to him? Does he remember that he once pledged to marry me when I was 40? Oh, I hope he has a LONG life with John, a LONG LIFE. I want him happy. (JPS journal, June 1, 1976)

☾   ☾   ☾

'Why aren't I enough?' she said. 'You are enough for me. I don't want anybody else but you. Why isn't it the same with you?'
'Having you, I can live all my life without anybody else, any other sheer intimacy. But to make it complete, really happy, I wanted eternal union with a man too: another kind of love,' he said. . . .
'You can't have two kinds of love. Why should you!'
'It seems as if I can't,' he said. 'Yet, I wanted it.'

(An exchange between Ursula and Birkin at the end of *Women in Love* by *DH Lawrence*, published in 1921)

☾   ☾   ☾

Bound up in secrets, Pete never kicked the habit of lying, even when he became happier. His lies were calculated omissions facilitated by his silence and his active choice to embrace ambiguity as a tool for communicating. When we were dating in the summer of 1972 in Chicago, he was involved with two other men. I did not realize the situation until my friend Paul revealed Pete's behavior to me in the summer of 1974. Since he was one of these two men, Paul knew more of the story.

It took me several years to accept that along with his gifts, Pete offered me lies. I knew everything was strange, and oddly exciting—late, unannounced visits, missed rendezvous, disappearances, and explanations that I questioned internally but accepted despite my doubts. I could never pin anything down since Pete was adept at lying. He was in control.

About this experience of Pete, I wrote:

> *The 'sickness' of Pete, or more accurately the extent of it, became apparent last night in a conversation with Paul.... Paul also began to explain how Pete had had 3 different stories for Dan, Paul, and me the summer of '72 (not to mention, naturally, all the other sets of lies he must have found necessary to tell). He slept with me and told me nothing, slept with Paul but told him that it was over with Dan, and slept with Dan but told him that ... Pete needed to help him [Paul]. Poor Pete and poor the three of us who trusted and believed him. Being gay or straight has very little to do with how you treat people, and it is quite obvious that Pete will never ever relate to people in a normal, good way.* (JPS journal, August 1, 1974)

Paul Preston and his partner Tim Lukaszewski, Fall 2017

Paul and I are close friends. He recently described Pete as *trying to keep everyone in their place/box, so none of us would ever have a chance to out Pete on his deceptions.* [PP email, October 2018]

Adrienne Rich describes the deep pain that follows anger when discovering a friend or lover has lied. The liar does not care nor foresee the consequence that we cannot stop doubting ourselves. It can take a long time to recover from deception from a loved one.

> *Why do we feel slightly crazy when we realize we have been lied to in a relationship? . . . When we discover that someone we trusted can be trusted no longer, it forces us to reexamine the universe, to question the whole instinct and concept of trust. For a while, we are thrust back onto some bleak, jutting ledge, in a dark pierced by sheets of fire, swept by sheets of rain, in a world before kinship, or naming, or tenderness exist; we are brought close to formlessness.*[13]

For a gay man in the 1970s and 1980s, it was not commonplace to be an out homosexual. Safe sex was to be in the future. Despite his characterization of the bar and cruise culture as "sordid and dehumanizing," Pete came to be an avid participant. He sought and found comfort, community, excitement, and meaning there.

During a visit to DC, Pete disappeared one night and did not return until the second morning with nary a phone call in between. He apologized.

> *I am still greatly ashamed of myself for abusing your hospitality during the last weekend I was in Washington, please understand that I had no intention of doing what I did when I left for the bars on Saturday night. However, that whole section of time turned out to be very therapeutic and even rewarding in that some of the people that I met that weekend have written to me here in Chicago. It would be easier to move to Washington [a change that*

---

13 Adrienne Rich (1929--2012), "Women and Honor: Some Notes on Lying." These notes were first read at the Hartwick Women Writers' Workshop at Hartwick College, Oneonta, NY, June 1975.

*he briefly considered] if I have a larger circle of friends. (*PJM
letter to JPS, December 21, 1979)

After another visit to DC, he sent me a thank you letter with this
anecdote.

> *Oh, yes, I was going to tell you about my train ride back to
> Chicago. To make things very short and leaving out a lot of the
> boring details, it boils down to this. I made friends with one of
> the railroad's service personnel almost before the train left the sta-
> tion and I did not have to spend the night sitting up in my seat.
> We've exchanged letters since then and he may be spending his
> vacation here in October. I can't say that it is really anything, but
> it sure does bolster my ever-sagging ego.* (PJM letter to JPS, July
> 15, 1980)

As I reread his letters, I noticed increasing content about his health. He
was an asthmatic and he had various long colds and then hepatitis in 1980.

> *It is mild enough as these things go. I spent ten days in bed with
> all sorts of rather unappetizing symptoms with which I shall not
> bore you. Mostly they run to a very bad case of the flu close upon the
> heels of which follows a very bad (or slightly bad, depending) case of
> jaundice. That is really the telltale symptom. Anyway, the jaundice
> is gone or almost gone and I am feeling remarkably fit. I still tire
> easily, but my appetite has come back with a vengeance and I am
> almost able to put in a full day's work. I suspect that this is Hepatitis
> A, the kind that comes from eating shellfish in months without 'r'
> rather than B, which is the kind most common to gay men. I won't
> know for sure until the lab results come back in another two weeks.
> By that time I should be almost over the damn thing–I hope. [Not
> sure if he ever told me what the labs revealed, at least, I don't have
> an explanation and I don't remember.]* (PJM letter to JPS, July
> 15, 1980)

He was in the hospital in January 1983. Before that, while vacationing in San Francisco, he was hospitalized for five days. In March, he wrote from the hospital in Chicago.

> *This siege is not severe but they, (the Dr.'s) decided to keep me over a day or 2 for some additional tests and observations. But then I have always thrived on being the ctr. of attn. & being waited on hand and foot. Other than these two recent, sudden episodes, things have been beautiful.* (PJM letter to JPS, March 18, 1983)

He offered lab test data, which, now years after the AIDS crisis, read all too clearly.

> *(1) I had a chronic low-level infection which was not being touched by the sorts of antibiotics which had been given me earlier. This left my lungs very sensitive to irritation which normally would not have bothered me. (2) I have allergies to more things than had been imagined. These were the things that evidently were constantly irritating me. Either environmental control (read better housekeeping) or desensitization should eliminate that problem. (3) I seem not to be producing some chemical in my body which is necessary to keep things going. This deficiency can be corrected by drugs which I am now taking. We are all hopeful that I shall not be bothered by this again, at least not very soon. (Medical people always hedge their bets.)* (PJM letter to JPS, April 14, 1983)

Pete's death was the first death of a friend, the first from AIDS, and the most significant. Like so many other LGBTQ people of my era, I have attended many memorials and funerals for people my age and younger. Too many.

My loss and the government's appalling refusal to recognize and address the epidemic were tough to experience. As a witness, I felt I could not scream loud enough. I began to develop a fresh voice by speaking out, confronting homophobia, and singing in the Lesbian & Gay Chorus of Washington, DC. In 1987, I quit a promising career path to work for myself. This choice gave me the ability to arrange my schedule around a full plate of volunteer commitments.

Pete's last letter is written in handwriting that I do not recognize.

March 6, 1986

Dear Tuli [I do not remember why he used this nickname for me. It might have had something to do with my unreadable penmanship/penwomanship.]

Please excuse the handwriting and/or spelling in this note. I still lack complete eye-hand-mind coordination and sometimes end up with strange words.

The azalea is most beautiful. It is impossible to tell you how many blossoms there are on the plant. It looks like over 50 and they are all gigantic. Both Jerry & I hope it will last a very long time. All who come into the room are amazed by its prodigious display.

Thank you also for your efforts to get me to Sanibel. [A friend of mine had offered her apartment in Sanibel, Florida, as a place for Pete to relax and recuperate after his stint in the hospital. He was able to go with his partner Jerry for a week.] *I look forward to ending my recuperation in a quiet, warm area. Jerry, of course, is looking for a more active vacation. I may just send him to Busch Gardens while I sunbathe. I understand that there are some nature preserves nearby–a bird sanctuary and something called Corkscrew swamp. Perhaps they will interest him for a couple of days. . . .*

I guess my recovery is moving smoothly. I've gain[ed] 5 lbs according to the nurse and she recommends that I drink beer in the evening to add calories. I think I shall follow her advice.

My lungs continue to be clear, which means the pneumonia has been completely eradicated.

I think I have nothing else at this end. The cherry blossoms must soon be out at the Tidal Pool [in Washington, DC]. Some-

day I shall see them. Probably after we have retired together. I hope your new office continues to please you. It will be a while before I get to see it but see it I will.

Take care of yourself. My best to your parents. I'm still working on finding a housewarming present for you, but I want it to be ideal.

Love, Pete

I received a chatty postcard from Sanibel and a housewarming gift, a crystal bookend shaped like a horse. It holds my heavier books in place.

Peter Meehan was employed as an administrative assistant to the manager of the Journals Division at the University of Chicago Press. He was an almost elfin Irishman[14] whose eyes really did twinkle and who had convictions about gay issues. One year he devoted an enormous chunk of accrued vacation time to the California political contests his friends were involved in. Then the time came to take on his own brave struggle with AIDS. We miss him. (Submitted on July 17, 1988, with Pete's panel for the AIDS Quilt, which was created by his friends. Written by Wayne T. Johnson.)

Entry from my journal, January 5, 1988:

It's just about the anniversary of Pete's death. I still cannot believe that he has gone, or as I sometimes think 'left me.' His love, his understanding were always there--no strings attached. Although not a part of my daily routine, he was always there to reassure me in a nonverbal way. Sometimes, I think of how we would snuggle together, sleep in each other's arms, and I am ashamed that I did not touch him more. It was hard to ignore the grotesqueness of his skin cancer--I could not kiss him. It was small of me. But now it's been one year. Only more loss awaits us and I refuse to believe that the meaning of life is this increas-

---

14 Pete was Polish and Irish. At the luncheon after his funeral, the restaurant's sound system played polkas over and over.

ing loss against which one attempts to build barricades which are weak in their very conception. But I don't know what else there is besides the fleeting moments of happiness. I miss Pete so much. If we weren't always in synch, we always counted on the other. It was understood, and acceptable in its understatement.

Lest we forget, silence = death. Or, as AIDS activist, songwriter, and singer Michael Callen (1955–1993) described this time period -- "This is Wartime."

**Pete's Panel as included in The Names Project
AIDS Memorial Quilt, c. 1988**

Just before my 70th birthday in August 2019, I planned a trip to Chicago to see my friend Mark Bowman (see chapter 10), who lives on the northwest side of the city. I had not visited my old town in about 20 years.

As I made my plans, I recognized a growing desire to visit Pete's grave, which, at first, I pushed away. I believe this life we have now is what there is. After that, dust. Pete is dust. Perhaps something exists for us after we check out, but I feel certain it is not anything that the human mind as presently constituted can construe with any certainty, much less maintain that anyone or any religious faith knows the truth.

Yet, I believe in the power of ritual, constructed by the human spirit as a tool for resolution. Pete and I had struggled to comprehend our relationship. I wondered if visiting him at his grave might seal that understanding for me, the one still living.

Even as my mind chided me that my special friend Pete would not be there, I asked Mark if he would visit Pete's grave with me. I had kept Pete's funeral prayer card, which listed the cemetery as Saint Adalbert in Niles, Illinois. I thought I remembered he was buried by a tree.

When I asked Mark for his help, he figured out the best way to Saint Adalbert, which required that we borrow a car from one of his daughters to drive north and a bit west. Saint Adalbert of Prague was born circa 956 and died on April 23, 997. He was the Bishop of Prague and a missionary to the Hungarians, Polish, and Prussians martyred in his efforts to convert Baltic Prussians to Christianity.

At the cemetery office, they gave us a map and directions to the Meehan family plot. Once we parked nearby, it took another 15 minutes to find the actual grave marker. Mark located it and called me over. There it was, Pete's grave. It looked like the picture on the cemetery website. It was unremarkable. His exact dates were not listed, only the months and years of birth and death. There was a smallish tree but I do not think it could have been there when he was buried in 1987. I learned his father had died at 65 within eight months of Pete and his brother died in 2009 at 60. His mother, having weathered the sorrow of losing two sons and her husband, lived to 91 and died in 2014.

I could not eek a spark of Pete's life from his gravestone. It provided facts but did not capture his spirit. That task is left to me and others who knew him. I can hold his brightness in my heart and acknowledge the impact he had on my life. Still missing you, Pete. Still here, Pete, partly angry at you, still furious at what happened to you, but a better person for knowing you and for remembering how you supported and loved me.

Not exactly signed, sealed, and delivered, but I accept my feelings.

☾   ☾   ☾

Of course, we [including BF John] would be very happy if you would visit. There should never be a question about that. You may want to bring your walking shoes and a hard hat, however. The annual Gay Pride Parade will be that weekend (Sunday) and I expect that I will be marching in it and I would be very happy if you would march with me. The hard hat may be necessary because the American Nazi Party has chosen to hold a 'Pro-Family, Anti-Homosexual Rally' to coincide with the event. . . . People are calling for non-confrontation but a group called The Stonewall Committee . . . is calling for open hostility. Since the police will be on hand to guarantee 'the peace,' and since they are not a particularly sympathetic bunch anyway, there may be trouble. I hope that it can be avoided. (PJM letter to JPS, May 22, 1982)

PETER J. MEEHAN
(February 26, 1948–January 11, 1987)

IMAGINE MY SURPRISE

1974–1978

AFTER MY year of independence in Strasbourg, France, and now armed with increased self-confidence, I returned to Syracuse University (SU) in August 1974, determined to complete a second year of coursework for my Ph.D. in the Department of Religion. I had spent the summer in Chicago, working, checking out my old haunts, and exploring my changing relationship with Pete, which was less intense but still important. My social life was at a lull.

To fund my expenses, I took a job as a resident advisor (RA) in the SU dorm system. It was a substantial package that covered tuition, room, board, and an annual $1,000 stipend. It was not a job that called to me, and I doubted I possessed the necessary traits of gregariousness, sociability, and empathy. As an introvert, I hoped that a steady, *laissez-faire* style on my part would click with my charges, as this style characterized by the RAs at the University of Chicago had worked for me as an undergraduate.

Winchell Hall, my dorm, named after Alexander Winchell, the first SU chancellor, was primarily a first-year women's dorm and the oldest dorm on campus. It was built of brick in 1900 and demolished in 1984. In 1974, the visible lack of any recent structural or furniture updates revealed its age. Fire escape ladders and landings cluttered the back of the building. Four stories high, it was perched on the edge of a hill at a traffic light that controlled the two major streets of the campus, University Avenue and Campus Drive. Winchell was a stone's throw to the campus and a few blocks from Marshall Street—nicknamed "M Street"—where there were student hangouts, restaurants, bars, and an excellent bookstore.

Students crammed the dormitory system that fall. Winchell housed an additional 30 women, which brought its head count to 90 instead of 60. The university had added a single bed, desk, and chest of drawers to each room to make them into triples. The university's calculation was that the dorms would clear out by the end of the first semester because of dropouts and because students would find alternative housing. In the meantime, the administration expected RAs to handle the overflow and the accompanying objections without complaint.

The RA apartment took up the space of several dorm rooms in the left corner on the first floor of the building, with an unavoidable view of the traffic light, which tiresomely discharged its duty of changing colors 24 hours a day. Besides the bed, the room's amenities included a private bathroom; a walk-in closet that I generously shared with a nest of large cockroaches; and a desk, telephone, and musty living room furniture that was reminiscent of the *pensions* I encountered when I was traveling in France, where dust rises from the pillows as one rearranges them before sleeping.

It was a privilege just to have somewhere to sit in addition to the bed and desk chair. It took some effort to annihilate the cockroaches, but once university maintenance accomplished their eviction, these were nice digs with more space than my Strasbourg studio. To enter or exit my apartment, one had to walk through the dorm's community space. At any hour there might be someone (or several people) sitting there. Likewise, at any hour, there might be a knock on my apartment door, a summons to which I was duty-bound to respond, even if it was simply a request for a new light bulb.

There was a staircase with 20 steps that connected the front hall to the entry door. The door was always locked but residents had keys. SU dorms were open to visitors 24 hours per day; the protocol was that residents were to greet their visitors at the front door. This proved to be a ridiculous expectation because visitors were not always expected. They could, and did, arrive at any time of the night or day, even from 10 pm until 3 am, when visitors finally went home to their own beds instead of seeking company. To help with this situation, there were several work study positions for hall monitors. With this coverage, as well as the efforts of assistant RA Thomasina Etheridge[15] and myself, the ever-ringing doorbell became less of a problem.

Radiators besieged Winchell. They gurgled, hissed, and banged loudly but did not produce significant heat. They were drained (bled is the rather striking technical term) periodically. They were an ongoing problem for Winchell residents and as a result, I was well known in the SU maintenance department, if only by my voice, because I was on the phone to consult about the radiators almost every single day of the work week. During the year, we had plumbing challenges, an awkward infestation of crabs that required disinfection of dorm toilets by yours truly, and several gas and water leaks. Early in my tenure, one resident who was an arts major, poured plaster-of-Paris down a sink in the first-floor communal bathroom, which sealed the drain. She was clearly repentant, and I protected her from being charged for the expensive repair by telling the maintenance department that I did not know who was responsible for the dastardly deed.

Before taking up my duties at Winchell, I attended a week-long orientation. There were various sessions about SU's history, the operation of the dorm, and policies governing the residential living system. One afternoon, a student health psychologist made a presentation about the issues that an incoming first-year student might face—homesickness, depression, excess consumption of alcohol (drugs were not yet a recognized issue), and difficulty with curriculum. Our psychologist alerted us that

---

15 Thomasina was a character and skilled at reading people. She lived on the fourth floor and kept a good eye on dorm happenings and personalities. One of her favorite expressions was, "When you've met the best, you can forget the rest."

some students could become inordinately attached to resident advisors. She advised us, as RAs and persons of power, not to confuse this attachment with friendship and to be careful in our response. It was important not to be perceived as having favorites among the students and to realize that the relationship between student and RA was not one of equality. (I am sure that the language of 1974 differed from what I wrote here, and that the psychologist was not intending to address romantic entanglements of the same sex variety.)

Loneliness afflicted me again, and I began falling down a rabbit hole. Since I had been away for a year, there were new graduate students in the Department of Religion. In the January--May 1973 semester, I had lived off-campus in a group house, and while I was in Strasbourg, those roommates had left Syracuse.

> *I'm drunk a little which takes care of the loneliness a little. I guess that's not so bad. Of late, I feel that ache again, and it's worse amidst the plentiful young—sort of nostalgia for a lost innocence or something.* (JPS journal, October 12, 1974)

I recognized that it took time for me to connect with others, just as it was in Cairo and boarding school. My seemingly serious personality and reserved temperament created a separation from the students for whom I was responsible. My supervisor was not helpful in suggesting techniques that might help in bridging this gap. In my formal evaluation with her, she concluded that my key problem was that I maintained "a distance from those around me." That was after she asked me if I came from a "close family." I thought she was a complete zero and suffered through our meetings with inwardly restrained exasperation. (JPS journal, November 21, 1974)

Yet, despite my reserved countenance, I did not seem to have a problem connecting with a returning sophomore who hailed from northern New York. She was part of a group of students who volunteered to help newbies move into their dorms, and she shared a room with two women on Winchell's top floor. I met her as she was carrying suitcases and boxes into the dorm before the start of classes. Her name was Lynne.

I was hard-pressed to look away from her luxurious brown hair, a hint of pink bubble gum in her mouth, her fun demeanor, and her aura of spontaneity. She stood out among the other 89 students in my charge. She was vibrant! She asked me lots of questions, not seeming to notice or care that she was flipping the RA–student relationship. Without apology, she put her cigarette out in her yogurt. Holy Moley, for some reason, that was exciting, and something I would never have done even if it had crossed my mind. She was more confident than I could ever imagine being. I should have been asking her questions, yet it always seemed to happen the other way around. I could not assert myself, and she enjoyed pushing my boundaries.

Lynne asked me one evening, when I was keeping her company at the hall monitor table at the top of the steps, "Have you ever thought about being a Lesbian?" I sensed danger and replied without hesitation, awkwardly and defensively, "I don't have to jump off a bridge to know what that feels like." Considering subsequent events, we have laughed about that exchange many times.

In my loneliness, I soaked up her attention while wondering from time to time, as expressed in my journal, whether my attraction, which I described as a "relationship/friendship," was appropriate. Lynne was 19, six years younger. I, too, was young in my unformed way, but I had a responsible position at the university.

If I didn't have Lynne, sometimes I wonder what I would do. I wonder whether the relationship/friendship with Lynne is really wise. For me it is an intense affair with disappointment when she finds her outlets elsewhere. Under her questioning, I find myself having to articulate a number of things and I am amazed that she cares. (Continuation of JPS journal entry of October 12, 1974)

Professional ethics emphatically suggest that my behavior was out of line and that I would be subject to discipline if university administrators uncovered my deception. I did not, or could not, think about repercussions. In those days, I was mostly heady, meaning I tried hard to keep my focus on my academic goals while fully engaging in breaking rules. Lynne's attention was a distraction that, I admitted, lifted me up in new ways. Talking with her was more appealing than studying, and I loved studying.

On weekends, Lynne and I drove around the Syracuse environs in my mustard-colored, stick-shift Gremlin—my first car, which I named Fred. It was a godsend to leave campus for a few hours. There was no cell phone to disturb, and the fall colors beckoned us. Fred offered privacy for Lynne and me and distance for me from the toil of running a dorm, for those duties were tiring. The city of Syracuse, cut through the middle by the eyesore known as Interstate 81, is not an enticing place, but there are many beautiful spots within short, driving distances and we went exploring as much as we could.

Imagine my surprise!¹⁶

> *No warts, no pangs of guilt after a couple of hours caressing and being caressed by Lynne. In some ways it seems a little innocuous this afternoon. But once I had admitted to myself and to her what I could not even write in here, I was relieved. Last evening, I spent some time reading 'The Love Song of J. Alfred Prufrock,'* ¹⁷ *and only today do I begin to understand why I am drawn to that line—'Do I dare disturb the universe?' Somehow, I felt as if we were making a leap together last night and that no matter what happened, neither she nor I would ever be the same. And, truth to tell, we aren't and haven't been for a while. Seems like I've been carrying Lynne around with me for weeks—she has always been close in mind if she has not been there physically. And I cannot deny that, nor do I want to. But this is all so odd to me. To feel so*

---

16 The name of a song and album by Holly Near that was released in 1993.
17 T. S. Eliot, "Do I dare/Disturb the universe? In a minute there is time/For decisions and revisions which a minute will reverse."

close, compatible, and so intense with a woman and to want her company more than anyone else's. I wanted to touch her hair and her hands for so long. (JPS journal, October 17, 1974)

Seems like Lynne was much more aware of our direction than I. I wonder at my repression (?) of my feelings for her and realize now that I ignored my journal for two months because I could not be honest in it. Yet, the signs were all there, flashing off and on, just like my traffic light. (JPS journal, November 12, 1974)

Like all fresh lovers, we were giddy and self-centered. In addition, our necessary secrecy forged a tight bond.

Sometimes I am amazed at how easy it was for me to make this 'radical' change. Easy, natural, and oh so right that I can't believe that loving a woman, loving Lynne, has anything at all to do with neuroses, with hating my father, with being disappointed in my sexual encounters with men or that it is a Condition (definitely with a capital 'C') which has to be cured. (JPS journal, December 5, 1974)

In our fledgling Lesbian relationship in 1974, we concealed what was happening to us. The high price of being out was unquestionable. When Lynne spent the night in my apartment, we figured out how she could exit my room without being seen. It meant rising early and trying to determine if someone was studying or sleeping in the community room outside my door. If I opened the door and saw someone, I pretended I had a reason to walk out my door and a reason to return almost immediately to my room. I am not a proficient liar, but I became quite practiced in this situation, particularly in applying the lie of omission.

The more troublesome part was figuring out a means of egress for Lynne. Our method of escaping detection involved a phone booth in a hallway outside the community room and away from the entrance to my apartment. I would call that phone from my room and invariably whoever was in the community room went and answered it. I hung up as soon as the person released the receiver from its cradle. Lynne took that opportunity to leave and head up the stairs to her room. She had a few close calls but always succeeded. I feel sure that her roommates already guessed what was happening, since Lynne spent many nights that fall away from her room. Lynne bore the biggest burden of sneaking around, as she was more likely than I to be seen and perhaps questioned by peers.

> *She leaves at 6:30 so we can retain our respectability, my job, our image.* (JPS journal, December 9, 1974)

These clandestine somersaults, as well as others, were thrilling and daunting and, while they cultivated an interdependence, they took a toll on us as well. It grew old for both of us to maintain a false pretense for the outside world about our relationship. The closet is both addictive and destructive. Addictive because of its secrecy but destructive because obeisance requires continuous false pretense.

> *I believe our relationship allows us to be what we are and to enjoy even difficult situations when we are together. No matter the situation, we can make the best of it. And yet I could not be here in this vomit pink room [my RA apartment] another day if I knew Lynne would be here next semester. I cannot conduct my life in secret, I cannot conceal what my happiness is, I have to be open. What does it mean to love if one is not freer in the process? And we are bound to society, for whatever reason one could name.* (JPS journal, December 6, 1974)

Looming large over our relationship was Lynne's semester abroad in Madrid, Spain, scheduled for the 1975 winter/spring semester. She would leave in January and return in May. The impending departure brought additional intensity:

> *The time of our leaving approaches. Lynne worries I hate SU and will not want to make a choice to remain there or that I*

will make the choice to remain, while I worry about her meeting
someone else in Spain. We both worry about our age difference. It
makes no difference when we are together—but Lynne must sam-
ple all that I did and maybe more. We both must have space to be
free. (JPS journal, December 1, 1974)

In our Winchell cocoon, we realized many residents suspected our secret, which threatened our safety. Lynne's time in Spain—briefly interrupted by a visit from me—was a good change for our relationship. It saved us
from SU administrators catching us in our lie, the potential consequences
of which would have been no small thing. Emotionally, it was healthy for
us to disengage a tad, although we kept up a busy correspondence.

For my parents, I contrived an explanation for my trip to Spain. Although I was not proud of my bald face lie, I told them I was attending a
conference in France, which sounded somewhat logical since I had spent
the previous academic year there.

On my way to Spain, I wrote a lengthy entry in my journal. I was ex-
cited but worried about money, and happy to be traveling to see Lynne,

> *. . . knowing that the urgency in me to see Lynne, which grows with*
> *every second of getting physically closer to her, would carry me forth.*
> *Standing on the platform for the train, a man gave me his*
> *unused ticket to NYC. It was meant to be. Well, whatever, it all*
> *soothed my Puritan conscience and it soothed that part of me which*
> *did not like lying to my parents. French club indeed! With time,*
> *it has become easier to talk, to say the words, to not worry about*
> *the reaction. But my parents are another matter, I have grown*
> *away from them this year, more perhaps than in the previous 5*
> *years combined. And yet our physical distance is less but having*
> *found Lynne and all she means to me, I feel the need of them less.*
> (JPS journal, February 28, 1975)

If Lynne had not entered my life, I would be much more conformist
in all things. I am not speaking only of Lesbianism. Her spirit guided us

as we broke society's rules and navigated our daily lives to see each other as much as possible.

Lynne was a preacher's kid (PK) and that, I discovered, meant she broke a lot of rules and rarely faced punishment. The latter was a totally foreign concept to me. I was in awe of her ability, and I was uncomfortably astonished to find that I, too, could break the bonds of convention without repercussions.

That fall semester was full of firsts for me. I asked for and received my first incomplete in a course. I sought temporary typing work as a Kelly Girl (KG) in violation of university regulations and the RA contract I had signed. I would use the illicit KG earnings to fund my two-week trip to Spain to see Lynne in March 1975, which meant that I would violate allowed excused absences from my dorm job. Thomasina was happy to cover for me. She, like Lynne, was someone less bound up in society's constraints.

> *What has become of the old academic Jill—Jesus, I didn't regret it at all [asking for the Incomplete]. I've whittled away the semester and could care less. I CARE NOT AT ALL. In fact, it made me laugh. I've waited 19-years to put my personal wishes ahead of academic demands. I rushed back to tell Lynne.* (JPS journal, December 10, 1974)

Lynne and I survived our separation during her time in Spain and the summer that followed when she worked at a resort in the Thousand Islands, NY, and I was studying for my comprehensive exams in DC. We were reunited in the fall of 1975. I was now the RA for Abrams Cottage, a much smaller, older-women's dorm for which I was much better suited.

> *Abrams causes me no problems. The women are all interesting and have extended themselves to me. At Winchell, I can never remember relaxing the first 3 weeks (if ever). But, here, I have felt no clash of my personality with anyone else.* (JPS journal, September 9, 1975)

Abrams' RA apartment was an upgrade from Winchell's, and it had no cockroach infestation. The radiators were in better shape and the duties lighter. The pay was the same. No longer were my comings and goings known to all, as my apartment had a separate entrance with a parking space for Fred. Lynne was living in an off-campus apartment. At Abrams, it was easier to be together; we could count on fewer unwanted interruptions. Lynne would prove to be the explorer; I was ready to settle down.

Lynne, ever the rule breaker, got a puppy, a beautiful, brindle puppy she named Margo. Margo was part Wheaten Terrier, part something else, and she was smart. She lived with Lynne but the two of them visited Abrams, meaning I broke another dorm rule with alacrity. That fall, the Department of Religion offered me a teaching assistant contract, and I moved out of Abrams in December, with great relief to give up being an RA, to a studio apartment on the west side of campus. Once again, I had escaped the unwanted revelation of various secrets that I was keeping close.

Lynne and I were each trying on different things, wanting to know who we were as individuals, to each other, and in the big world. There were few obvious role models.

Well, Rita Mae Brown[18] ain't got the answers either. I'm not a man-hater and I don't feel so alienated from the system that I see no possibilities within it. I can't be a woman-hopping Lesbian, I can't view this as a new sexual experiment. I'm involved with Lynne. Oh, we've been less than happy together these past few days—trying to define our relationship, trying (at least I am) to let go, to give her freedom. Whatever it is in me which makes me grab, clutch I haven't conquered yet. I want very much to understand it. Being alone is infinitely less complicated and yet not satisfying. Oh, what am I? A child, a woman: a Lesbian, a straight? In the car last night, Lynne asked me 'Do you like yourself?' Ah, some memories appeared with that one. Still working

18 *Rubyfruit Jungle* by Rita Mae Brown was essential reading for women who were discovering that they loved women. I read it in fall 1974.

*it out—still trying to deal with emotions of inadequacy, of para-
noia, of doubt. And I suppose it shall ever be thus.* (JPS journal,
November 23, 1974)

What we were doing was illegal and we, ourselves, were illegal for
loving each other. To be together, we were forced to be clandestine, but
this hardly diminished our individual desires to know more about the
counterculture we had entered together.

☾   ☾   ☾

Ever the aspiring academic, and in a bold, personal move, I looked
up "Lesbian" in SU's Bird Library. The card catalogue revealed several ti-
tles—no more than five—including *The Ladder*, the first nationally dis-
tributed Lesbian publication in the United States. Published from 1956
to 1972, it was the primary communication method for the Daughters
of Bilitis (DOB), the first Lesbian organization in the US.[19] *The Ladder's*
message was that women-loving-women were not alone. It strengthened
the message and built community through its poetry, short stories, and
essays. In San Francisco, gatherings of the DOB were an alternative to
the bars where gays and Lesbians risked arrest.[20]

I did not have sufficient daring to subscribe to *The Ladder.* My personal mail was not private in the dorm since work-study students distrib-
uted the mail. I did venture each month to Achilles (as we called it), the
lefty bookstore on Marshall Street, to pick up a copy of "off our backs"
(also known as "oob"), a radical, Lesbian newspaper published out of
Washington, DC. One of my first temp job assignments in DC was at a
think tank. My supervisor for the week was Carol Anne Douglas, whose
columns I had read in "oob." I was in awe of her confidence and position.

19 Wikipedia. "Bilitis" was the name of a fictional Lesbian contemporary of Sappho. The name was
obscure and its use by the DOB allowed for a cover for their activities. In its mission statement, The
Ladder promoted the "Education of the variant" and advocated for a mode of behavior and dress
acceptable to society.

20 Note from Editor: Because I was curious, I looked up "Lesbian" in the University of Michigan
Library catalog search. I received 12,051 results in the library's catalog, almost 3 million articles, 31
databases, and a link to contact the librarian specializing in gender and sexuality studies. (Daniel
Weaver 2020)

For the five days of my assignment, I tried to find the guts to come out to her but failed.

The discovery of *Our Bodies Ourselves*, an informative, affirming guide to women's reproductive health and sexuality, first published in 1970, answered a lot of questions. It provided information that my mother, born in 1907 and who came of age in the mid-1920s, never told me, and most likely did not know herself, at least, not in the graphic detail provided by *Our Bodies Ourselves*.

By the time I was consulting the card catalogue, I had unknowingly begun my education as a "variant" (to apply a label from the DOB) by reading relevant books and keeping a list of them in the back of my journal. They revealed my growing curiosity about women's roles and alternative relationships. From July 1973 through December 1974, I perused works by Simone de Beauvoir (the first two volumes of her memoir), Virginia Woolf, H. Montgomery Hyde (*The Other Love*), Nigel Nicolson (*Portrait of a Marriage*), Anais Nin's diaries, and the rollicking and raw *Rubyfruit Jungle* by Rita Mae Brown. As an example of the changes in the world, I recently found a paperback copy of Brown's iconic novel in a Little Free Library in my neighborhood. I had no problem pulling it out and carrying it home in my hands to be reread. Nothing like that could have happened to me in the 1970s in Syracuse.

The heroine of *Rubyfruit Jungle*, the independent Molly Bolt, follows a circuitous route to realizing her romantic and professional dreams. She is an adopted child of a poor family in Florida, who has her first same-sex experience in sixth grade and continues her explorations, sometimes sleeping with men as well. Since the novel's publication in 1973, Molly's story has achieved iconic status as essential reading for women who love women. Molly's struggles resonated with me because there were few public examples of her pluck when I was coming out.

It is not recorded on my list, but I remember reading Jill Johnston's *Lesbian Nation* when I returned to Washington, DC, in 1974 for December holidays with my parents. The book's cover radiated the title in bold print, and I simultaneously relished and worried about the telegraphing of its unmistakable message. I made a conscious choice to leave the book on my bedside table. Part of me was trying to leave a helpful clue for my parents but they did not take my bait.

In 1970s Syracuse, Lynne and I continued the search begun by the DOB for people like ourselves and for sisters who might be simpatico. We did not know any. I did not always like nor trust the few Lesbians I met, nor did I cleave to the Lesbian culture that was revealed in underground newspapers and magazines. I encountered intense emotional reluctance as I made my way. I longed to embrace Lynne but was much slower to take up the Lesbian subculture, which included rules and edicts that were alien to me.

My growing Feminism facilitated my entry into Lesbianism. Feminism opened my thinking about fresh roles for women and new possibilities for relationships. I certainly thought that to be a Lesbian was to be a Feminist and vice versa. But Lesbianism and Feminism are not the same, although common parlance in the 1970s might have implied that they are. These two states of being and activism had a complex, overlapping connection that resisted easy explanation. In coming out, I discovered many Lesbians were also separatists, and even if they were not, the term was used against them.[21] I began to read the work of Feminist poet Adrienne Rich on these conflicts.

> . . . *even for lesbians, the word* **lesbian** *has many resonances. Some of us would destroy the word altogether. Others would transform it, still others eagerly claim and speak it after years of being unable to utter it. Feminists have been made to fear that they will be 'discredited' if perceived as lesbians; some lesbians have withdrawn or been forced into non-feminist enclaves (such as the 'gay' movement) which reject and denigrate 'straight' women.*[22]

As a Brownie, I had "flown up" to become a Girl Scout. A similar ritual beckoned to me as an inexperienced Lesbian, although it was much more uncomfortable to contemplate. I seriously worried that I would have to sleep naked in the woods under the full moon with similarly *de-*

---

21 With thanks to Adrienne Rich's discussion of this topic in a 1976 essay, "It Is the Lesbian in Us."
22 Ibid.

shabillée women to prove my Lesbianism. Nonmonogamy seemed to be the preferred social status and practice for many Lesbians. A symbolic badge-of-courage awaited the Lesbian who ceased to shave her legs *and* her underarms. Hairy armpits indicated a Lesbian who leaned to the militant side of things, sometimes characterized as "granola." She often had short hair, too. Lipstick Lesbians, who had a later coming out, eschewed the dressed-down attire that many of us adopted as a uniform and lavender clue to others like us.

In college, I signed up with trepidation for a poetry class with Henry Rago, a poet and editor of *Poetry* magazine. I met with him privately because his assignments puzzled me. What was the task? He advised I pick up a book of poetry and after touching it and looking it over, open to any page and begin reading. If I felt no resonance with what I read, he advised to try another page, so on and so on. He was confident that I would soon find some words to read. He believed, "Give yourself up to poetry and it will find you." Mr. Rago died suddenly in the early spring of 1969. He was young, 53, and I was very sad to go to class to find a substitute professor.

Mr. Rago's guidance steered me to poetry as a place of inspiration and solace. I began with e. e. cummings and worked my way to T. S. Eliot and others, including Sylvia Plath and Anne Sexton. I continue to read and enjoy poetry in the Henry Rago manner and now, I write haiku.

Somewhere in my readings, I discovered that Adrienne Rich was a Lesbian and I sought her poetry. Her words were helpful in identifying the challenges behind choices I was facing and making. Her essays became more important to me than her poetry.

> *We have been expected to lie with our bodies: to bleach, redden, unkink or curl our hair, pluck eyebrows, shave armpits, wear padding in various places or lace ourselves, take little steps, glaze finger and toe nails, wear clothes that emphasized our helplessness. We have been required to tell different lies at different times, depending on what the men of the time needed to hear.*[23]

---

23 Adrienne Rich, 1975 essay, "Women and Honor: Some Notes on Lying."

In the Lesbian world, there was an acknowledgment of class difference; for example, it was not unusual when purchasing a concert ticket to be asked to state your income. This consideration was new to me. Unlike my own experience of close friendships with Peter and Pete, Lesbians did not have close relationships with men. Some latitude existed for male family members and gay men. Partnered Lesbians (it seemed to me) negotiated the minutest details of their relationships at the cost of their happiness. Since I had little experience with successful intimate relationships, I now recognize my judgment in my observation.

> *I contemplate going to the Lesbian Feminist meeting tonight. The thought scares me. Why? I've tried to analyze it—because it's a group, because my cover will fade for some, because I'm afraid of being attracted to other women, and yet want it very much. . . . I feel I must push myself to go. I don't know whether tonight's the night, but I must go some time.* (JPS journal, July 8, 1976)

The next day, in a long journal entry, I reported attending the meeting the previous evening.

> *It's hard to imagine what made me so nervous about going in the first place, although, today, it seemed dream-like that I had been there. The group is highly political, and if I were to become a regular, I think it would be difficult to retain any anonymity. They were friendly, but not effusive. . . . Once again, the short hair. Once my initial nervousness faded, I relaxed and enjoyed the humor. . . . I think membership in the group demands a kind of commitment and statement that I'm not ready to make, nor may ever be ready to make. I want to make sure that my life is <u>open</u>, if only because there are men in the world and no matter what I do, I am going to have to continue to deal with them on at least a superficial level. . . . Somehow I found it easier to deal with the male world today. Good thing too, because the male sex surrounded me all day.* (JPS journal, July 9, 1976)

Following rules was important to me, ingrained from birth. Although I broke a Big Rule by entering the Lesbian counterculture in the first place, I experienced an uneasy dissonance with its precepts. Early on, I sensed I could not follow the Lesbian rules to the letter. I had left one set of axioms for another, but, in a reverse twist, I found a set of an equally demanding canon to achieve conformity and acceptance. These new-to-me rules felt very rigid. Lynne's embrace of this new world in a bigger, less-hesitant way signaled a deepening divide between us and portended the inevitable break-up of our relationship.

It did not occur to me that I could continue to pick and choose who I wanted to be, even going to the point of rejecting Lesbian rules for something else. It was a paradox.

☾   ☾   ☾

Despite my love for Lynne, I did not have the emotional maturity to trust her completely, which became a problem as our relationship moved from the giddy stage to its next phase (for which I do not have a catchy name). In previous relationships, I called myself the "clutcher," the person who was suspicious of the other's commitment, particularly when I sensed emotions shifting or cooling. My stomach would roil around, and eating was difficult. My controlling instincts came to the fore and propelled me into a repetitive, torturous circle of suspicion, jealousy, anxiety, paranoia, guilt, and, sometimes, reconciliation. These emotions shaded many other relationships that ended in both acrimonious and amiable break-ups. On occasion, my emotional paranoia proved to be justified, and the pattern hardened; there are cheaters in the world. I have lived long enough to count myself among them. Honesty to oneself and to others is difficult to achieve in the absolute.

In my journal, I find this passage:

It is my own feeling of inadequacy which will push us apart
sooner than anything else. Somehow, I just can't seem to grasp that

> *Lynne loves me the best way I have ever been loved. Do I want to own her? What is it which tears at me so? The inevitability of her seeking someone else, of not including me somehow, the inevitability of her independence from me? Jesus, I am so screwed up. Why do I insist upon chipping away at what we have? I must be strong. I must be strong enough to stand beside her. I must not fear her shutting me out but must respect it.* (JPS journal, September 24, 1975)

Student health provided free mental health counseling, so I decided to try it out. I got what I paid for. Miss Woodford, a graduate student in psychology, was my therapist. Student health guidelines prohibited the use of her first name. It was a learning experience for both of us, as I believe I must have been one of her first clients and she was my first therapist.

The gentle whirring sound of a reel-to-reel tape recorder accompanied my sessions. I consented to this intrusion but still it was daunting to realize that my words were being taped for posterity, or at least for clinical purposes. In stating my purpose for seeking therapy, I revealed I was in love with a woman and wanted to understand what was happening. In my third or fourth session, in any case, my last session, Miss Woodford asked me to describe the qualities I was seeking in my ideal man. I took a deep breath and reminded her I was in love with a woman.

To let Miss Woodford off the hook to a small degree, I was an ingenue as a Lesbian and inexperienced when it came to understanding myself. I held mostly unquestioned conventional norms richly flavored with self-righteousness and judgment. These norms were problematic when I tried to manage power within a relationship of supposed coequals. They required some extensive unpacking. I found success in that endeavor with more experienced therapists who helped me understand that I am not the sole person contributing to my relationships; their construction belongs to the parties involved.

The main benefit of therapy was that it allowed me to own my Lesbian relationship with an undergraduate woman six years younger. It is strange to me now to realize that Miss Woodford and I spent little time discussing Lynne's and my age difference, particularly since it would have been a strong entry point into my actions. My self-image relied on my tightly held assurance of my maturity, although my intimate involvement with a college sophomore was an obvious challenge to that perspective. I had qualms about the six-year age gap, which I believed arose from embarrassment, not ethical concerns. That I did not wield my power inappropriately did not cause the inequity to vanish. If not for patient confidentiality, Miss Woodford should have reported me, and I would have lost my job and perhaps my graduate student status, as well.

It was five years later when I fully realized that Lynne's and my relationship was ethically compromising. The professional world I entered after graduate school revealed the power that men possessed and exercised because they were in charge. Any interest that a man took in a woman's career was helpful but it also often carried other expectations. I had experienced a taste of this as a graduate student but in the culture of the nonacademic professional world, sexual harassment suddenly came into clear focus for me. The term "sexual harassment" was coined in 1975 but its behavior is ageless.

In the early 1980s, a younger colleague told me of an experience with the senior general counsel for our trade association. He was the treasured right hand to the president and his advice was of paramount importance to the organization. During an annual convention, the lawyer came to her hotel room on a work pretext. When she opened the door, he asked for entrance, which she denied. After listening to her story, I pressed her to report his misconduct to the president but she declined. My argument was that the lawyer misused his power in relationship to her by asking for a sexual encounter and presuming that his status would protect him from any objections she might register. He had no concerns unless she reported him. The lawyer continued his successful career. I heatedly pointed out that he might have behaved similarly in the past and that her silence would contribute to future, similar behavior. We are still friends but we have never again discussed this topic.

Mostly, I was a single Lesbian from 1978 to 1996, and I had an impossibly difficult time asking another woman out on a date; it was entrenched in me to be passive, that is, to wait for an invitation. I experienced many long waits. It turns out that I was not alone in this predicament, although I did not know it then. Lesbian lore is rife with stories about coffee dates—

the point of these was to meet in a neutral space and then figure out at another time whether the coffee date was, or could foster, a "real date." I went on many coffee outings at all times of the day but rarely knew whether I was on a date. Another staple of Lesbian lore are jokes about U-Hauls.[24]

The first time I asked my partner Jane out on a date in 1996, I had to muster a steely determination to make my intentions clear. She declined the invitation because she did not understand I was asking her out; instead, she thought I was letting her down easily. I found the nerve to pose the question again, pointedly using the word "date," and that worked!

But back in Syracuse, Lynne and I were merely searching for women who were like us. Lynne had her ear tuned to the Lesbian grapevine, which alerted her to a bar outside Syracuse called The Laurel Tree. During the week, it was the Sportsmen's Inn. Lynne suggested we check it out and I hesitantly agreed, not knowing what to expect. Before we went inside, I sat crying in the car while Lynne assured me that all would be well. The airy bar was drab and a bit of a let-down after my embarrassing hysteria. There were Lesbians inside, and shockingly, nothing happened to us.

Another time, we went to a women's bar in Chittenango, NY,[25] about 15 miles from Syracuse, in the company of Kit Havice, an associate professor in the Department of Religion, and her partner Pan. Lynne had cultivated her own friendship with them while I removed myself because I was not their fan and Kit was a faculty member in my department. Despite these complications, I was part of the evening and enjoyed myself in the company of other Lesbians.

Afterwards, I wrote:

> *It was a rather small bar filled with women, women far removed from Gucci bags. They were mostly professionals, of all ages and shapes, and they were just having fun. There was nothing fearful about it, and I enjoyed myself thoroughly. There must be*

24 If you do not know what I am referencing, ask a Lesbian who is 55 or older. There is bound to be one in your neighborhood.

25 Chittenango, NY, is the birthplace of Lyman Frank Baum, author of the *The Wizard of Oz*. The town is given over to the movie. At our brief and in-the-dark visit, I was unaware of the strong connections of gay culture to the movie and Judy Garland. Ironic, that. Chittenango's population as of the 2010 US census was 5,081.

lots of us around, and yet in Syracuse it's hard to believe that there
are many Lesbians. Last night was an eyeopener in that respect.
(JPS journal, March 21, 1976)

In 1973, before meeting Lynne, I had struck up a friendship with Dan Smith, a professor of Hinduism and Asian religions in the Department of Religion. As a scholar and pioneer of the study of Hindu popular culture, Dan was a documentary filmmaker, author, and collector of Indian art. We had an age gap of 21 years but we connected when I took his class featuring classic Asian texts, and I helped with the undergraduates. Dan had a pleasant, appealing countenance, and I loved talking with him. He would treat me to ice cream cones at the local Carvel and to infrequent but delicious dinners. He was always a generous listener, and he patiently heard me out whenever I became frustrated with his professional home and employer, the Department of Religion.

Several times, I asked him for a loan of $20 and each time he smiled, opened his wallet without hesitation, and gave me the money, no questions asked. He was familiar with the traumatic life of a graduate student.

I suspected he was gay; he had mentioned his roommate, whom, to my Lesbian ear-in-training, sounded more like a partner. That impression was reinforced when I visited their beautifully furnished and decorated home several times. Once they were working together in the garden, describing to Lynne (who had come along) and me how they were planting a border of trees at the back of the big lot to create privacy and beauty. The planting of these young trees was a sign of their expectation of longevity together. I longed to begin a shared life with Lynne.

Still, Dan, as charming and wonderful as he was, was a man and a professor and not likely to know what Lesbians were doing for fun.[26] We came out to each other after I left Syracuse and our friendship solidified. We had many happy times together, particularly around celebrations of our September birthdays, and I got to know his life partner and husband Coy Ludwig, the aforementioned roommate. Dan was a substantial support to me when I came out to my parents. Dan passed away in October 2013 at 85.

---

26 Coy would have known, since it turns out that he was thoroughly connected to the gay /Lesbian life in upstate NY. But it never crossed my mind to ask him. Coy has become a close friend.

H. Daniel Smith c.1970

Via the postal service, my college roommate Amy sent word that she had fallen in love with a woman. This was extraordinary news—the kind that made Lynne and me shout for joy. Amy visited me in Syracuse early in the fall of 1975, and she met Lynne.

> *A letter from Amy last week had the 3 of us (LJB, JPS, and Margo) happy as could be. I still can't get over it, Amy is in love with a woman. Amy wrote me a letter in which she told me I was important to her. It's a good thing I'm not there or I'd want to hug her, and somehow, I don't think she's quite ready for that. But the vision I have in my head of Amy giggling, writing love letters, etc.—it's so amazing.* (JPS journal, October 26, 1976)

Amy was a reserved brainiac with a buried wit; we had a good time living together in Chicago. Our friendship never seemed to include private exchanges about relationships, and I do not recall Amy ever having a romantic interest. It was splendid news to make this connection with someone whom I knew well and whose judgment I respected. That Amy was living in Denver, 1,600 miles away, was not a deterrent for Lynne and me; instead, it fueled us in our quest to be with other Lesbians.

We immediately decided to drive to Denver over our spring break holiday in March 1977. After putting together 10 days for the drive and visit, without skipping classes or obligations, we packed up Fred and headed off. Sensibly, we borrowed a cooler from Dan for food and drinks to keep expenses down. Margo went with us. For long periods of time, she stood on the back seat and put her head between the two "bucket" seats (the bucket seats in the Gremlin were not true bucket seats, but I digress and quibble). She's a bit like a friendly cow, we thought and laughed. We sang to Margo to pass the time—Fred's radio had died some time before. Our travel went well until we hit a spring snowstorm in Nebraska, which required an extra night's expense in a motel, but we got to Denver. We met Amy's partner Lea Ann and other Lesbians, all on the "granola" side, we whispered to each other, although they could have been a reflection of the casual style of the West rather than making a political statement. The trip buoyed us because we met women like ourselves. We now knew for sure that they were out there.

Women's music—music by women, for women, and about women—was a rising cultural phenomenon that even made its way to Syracuse. In 1972, Maxine Feldman recorded the first Lesbian record album, "Angry Atthis"; Atthis was the lover of Sappho. Lynne went to a Cris Williamson concert in Syracuse and excitedly reported back about the music and all the women in the audience. This was great news that there were lots of Lesbians there! Williamson's first album, "The Changer and the Changed," was released in 1975 and it became a Lesbian classic, particularly the first song, "Waterfall," which describes women-loving women beautifully and melodically. Its lyrics likening women loving women to the sensation of water falling over water still speak to Lesbians today.[27] The existence of women's music was communicated by word-of-mouth and, for some, women's music meant "Lesbians are found here." It was the truth.

Trapped in Syracuse, we knew that Washington, DC, was gaining a reputation for its receptiveness to gay and Lesbian people, but we were not fully aware of the city's major changes to discriminatory practices

27 Lyrics and music by Cris Williamson.

and laws. When visiting in spring 1976, we found Club Madame, which was touted in *Gaia's Guide* as the hottest Lesbian bar on the East Coast. Upon entering, we discovered the club had become a drag bar, presumably since the publication of the Guide. The DC Gay and Lesbian Activists Alliance (GLAA), founded in 1971, was already working to secure gay and Lesbian rights for DC citizens. Frank Kameny (1925–2011), who was an early, significant leader for gay rights, had founded a DC chapter of the Mattachine Society in 1961 to protest the arbitrary firing of federal employees because of sexual orientation.[28] We picked up copies of *The Washington Blade*,[29] the longest-running gay newspaper in the country.

Lynne and I moved to Washington, DC, in the fall of 1977, because our minimal research and our guts suggested that we could live more openly there. There was a gay newspaper, a gay bookstore, and a women's bookstore. We did not have jobs, but we rented an apartment by borrowing $500 from my parents to cover the security deposit and one month's rent. Lynne immediately became a successful salesperson at a VW dealership, and I took up the toil of a temporary secretary before landing a full-time gig at a national trade association. Through Lynne's sales work, we met several Lesbians—a single Lesbian who was a lawyer at the Justice Department and a couple who had moved to the area about the same time as we did. From there, our pool of people-like-us grew larger and larger. A good, male friend also surfaced in DC at the same time and revealed he was gay. The possibilities were many in our new, more accepting environment.

It was not yet possible to be an out Lesbian in the working world, as my failed experience coming out to Carol Anne Douglas had demonstrated. It was easier to be in DC than in Syracuse because in a bigger city I could maintain a life for the outside world and another for an inside world where Lynne and I socialized with Lesbians and frequented the few Lesbian bars. I did not realize that I would have to be my Own Lesbian, the subject of many journal entries.

28 Harry Hay founded the Mattachine Society in 1950 in LA to protect the rights of gay men.
29 Lynne is now the publisher of *The Washington Blade.*

Lynne responded excitedly to the pull of exploration whereas my introverted self slowly retreated, relying on Lynne to build our social connections. I struggled to understand the contents of the package that I had opened excitedly and with little thought--Lesbian life. My life would become but one example.

> *I came to the realization that in becoming more and more 'attached' to Lynne, I once again lost my own sense of self as she must have lost hers. And now, in our detaching I gain myself back again. If we can somehow remain detached and each inwardly whole, we will indeed build something better than we had before. Because in the building we will both be growing together and separately, being ourselves individually, not Lynne+Jill or Jill+Lynne. We will not lose our own sense of self, a product of attachment. Detachment+Growth—Possible? There will be no need for Sacrifice—Allelulia!* (JPS journal, July 8, 1976)

Lynne and I, our love story, experienced a drawn-out denouement. We came to accept that we were on different paths. She was not satisfied as being half of a settled couple; she wanted a wider world, perhaps one that did not presume monogamy. I was not on that train.

> *Berkeley House—I was recalling the first time I stayed here [around Fall 1978] when I was so upset about Lynne. I wrote in my journal that there would be a long unravelling of our relationship and I was right. Long unravelling, now a rebuilding. She and I are pretty neat as far as our relationship goes.* (JPS journal, November 20, 1980, perhaps written in California*)*

We did what people do in an irreconcilable situation where there is strong emotional attachment. We argued, we reconciled, we tried accommodations for the other's point of view, we argued again, we hurt the other, and we were sad. I was angry for a long time. We were young without support and with limited life skills, but we eventually achieved a meaningful rapprochement. We let go, relaxed, bonded through our memories, grew to trust each other, and laughed—actions that would have been helpful in building a lasting romantic partnership.

In our special friendship, we are familiar with each other's lives but we pursue separate paths that occasionally connect. We know we are solid and can depend on the other. We have mourned the loss of the other's parents, friends, and dogs, and shared the joys of the other's life. I never imagined such a peaceful and satisfying ending to this love story. I never imagined that I could write it down with joy in my heart. It is a gift for a lifetime.

Imagine my surprise.

☾   ☾   ☾

Friendship uniquely requires mutual self-knowledge and will. It takes two competent, willing people to be friends. You cannot impose a friendship on someone, although you can impose a crush, a lawsuit, or an obsession. If friendship is not reciprocated, it simply ceases to exist or, rather, it never existed in the first place. (Andrew Sullivan, Love Undetectable: Notes on Friendship, Sex and Survival, 1998)

Lynne J. Brown, September 1983

DEAR DEPARTMENT OF RELIGION

1975–1977, 2018–2019

October 1, 2018

Dear Department of Religion, Syracuse University:

I received my Ph.D. from the Department of Religion in 1981.

I also received some life lessons while studying for my Ph.D. One of them was being sexually harassed by Professor DB Robertson in 1975. I reported this incident to Dr. Ron Cavanagh, Chair of the Department. I met with Robertson and Cavanagh at Cavanagh's office. Robertson forcefully denied any inappropriate behavior on his part. The Committee for Graduate Studies, at the request of Dr. Cavanagh, allowed me to minimize my encounters with Robertson, including a mid-semester rearrangement of my classes. I did not pursue any further action against Robertson. I left Syracuse in the fall of 1977 and completed the requirements for my Ph.D. from Washington, D.C.

This is but one complaint, but I know there were other instances of sexual harassment by professors teaching in the Department of Religion during my time in Syracuse and at SU (1974--1977), although I don't believe they were reported. Even recognizing the difference in cultural and organizational mores between the 1970s and now, I believe the department harbored a culture of sexual harassment, even if it did not actively encourage it.

I am writing to the Religion Department now because I want to make sure that this incident is recorded in the history of the department. Perhaps, it already is and has been responsible, in some small part, for increased enlightenment about these issues over time.

If at all helpful, I am willing to discuss in more detail what happened. I kept a journal.

Thank you for reading.

Sincerely,

Jill P. Strachan, Ph.D.

Thirteen months later, October 30, 2019, I had received no response.

I pursued doctoral studies in the Department of Religion at Syracuse University (SU), and lived in Syracuse from 1974 to 1977, completing my PhD dissertation after I moved to Washington, DC. In 1981, I was awarded a Doctor of Philosophy degree, my PhD.

It was a long road: two years of coursework and independent study besides coursework already completed for a master's degree. Other hurdles included comprehensive exams on completed studies, research for a dissertation topic, writing the dissertation, and an oral defense before a committee of professors (who also have jumped through all these hoops at some point and received a PhD). Until the degree is conferred, someone who has passed comprehensive exams and whose dissertation proposal has been accepted is called a PhD Candidate.

It took me 10 years to complete the process. In that decade, there were two years when my academic work was on the back burner while I started a new, Lesbian life in a big city and happily applied myself to a nonacademic career. I credit my first boss after academia, Chuck Carey, for encouraging me to ride the PhD path to its ultimate destination. He offered flexibility in my work schedule as his executive assistant at the National Food Processors Association, which was not the norm for the early 1980s. Chuck was the first person I called when I successfully completed my oral defense.

There are many candidates who do not complete the process; they are called ABDs (all but dissertation). Getting even that far is an accomplishment, as the path is full of challenges and pitfalls. Dissertation advisers can be helpful, generous, thoughtful, eager to mentor and guide, but they can be competitive, uncaring, and ego-driven at the expense of the advisee. Candidates must pick an adviser carefully and strategically.

The personal can play a decisive role in the quest for a PhD. Success can rise and fall on the personal relationship with one's adviser. If the adviser and candidate do not have good chemistry and understanding, they will struggle throughout the process. Emotions, pleasant or otherwise, can be projected onto the candidate.

When I began my studies in the early 1970s, the study of religion was shifting away from the structure of traditional divinity schools, which emphasized religious faith and training for a clerical life. My interest in religion arose from my childhood abroad, where I learned about non-Christian cultures, faiths, and history. To study religion, I could apply to a divinity school, expecting that the prevailing point of view would reflect Christianity and training for a pastoral career. My other options included history programs or departments of religion, such as SU's, whose mission was broad and flexible.

My undergraduate degree at the University of Chicago was in the history and philosophy of religion. I also completed a one-year master's program in general studies of the humanities so that I could continue to study religion while feeding an additional interest in American culture. SU offered a wider vision for my studies because the department was interested in the connections between religion and culture and social issues and politics. The tools were traditional but there was latitude for constructing an individual approach.

The current statement of scope on SU's website is:

> *The Department of Religion . . . emphasizes cultural and the-*
> *oretical approaches to the study of religion and draws attention to*
> *the relationship of religion with literature, art, history, psycholo-*
> *gy, politics and philosophy. Students are encouraged to investigate*
> *both the religious dimensions of secular culture (film and music,*
> *for example) and traditional religions as cultural phenomena.*

The language and description are familiar. Subject areas for my five comprehensive exams were Early Christianity, American Transcendentalists, Islam, William Faulkner, and the prospectus for my proposed dissertation topic, "Richard Nixon: Representative Religious American." The successful completion of the exams illustrated proficiency for topics and a facility to discuss various scholarly perspectives as well as my personal conclusions. My work on Richard Nixon would still conform neatly into the department's concept of studies in religious studies. This fit was the primary reason I was happy to be at SU. I judged I had found a comfortable intellectual home to support my interests and thinking.

Or so I thought.

Despite my family's disappointment, I did not attend the graduation ceremony for my PhD. I had sufficient pride in my accomplishment that I had my diploma framed, which was not cheap. Yet, it is leaning against a wall in my closet, invisible behind hanging clothes.

Since my third year in college, I had wanted to teach at the college I held an idyllic view of the academic life and profession.. Although academic life was a goal that I seriously pursued, my zest for academic study faded away. Circumstances and fortune took me on a different path.

℀   ℀   ℀

Here is my story.

Principal characters: Dr. DB Robertson, Dr. Ronald Cavanagh, and me. (DB, RC, and me.)

In 1975, Dr. DB Robertson (DB, never D.B.), a tenured professor, had been teaching in the department for a long time. He primarily taught undergraduates but an occasional graduate student sought him out for independent study. He attended many department events (meetings and social occasions) and was always eager to have a conversation. DB seemed to be the logical choice for my dissertation advisor; our research interests in American history and social issues were aligned and we both studied religion through a political lens rather than the more traditional study of religion of specific faiths.

Dr. Ronald Cavanagh (RC), chair of the department, had overall responsibility for the students and faculty in the department.

Jill Strachan, potential PhD candidate in spring of 1975, was close to completing two years of coursework for my PhD. My thoughts turned to selecting my dissertation adviser, the all-important, trusted (here's hoping) person who would guide me through my research and the various hoops that I would face in completing and defending my dissertation. At that point, I planned to finish the process in another two years. I was taking one class and an independent study with DB, which amounted to two-thirds of my coursework for that semester. I was also preparing to take five comprehensive examinations.

There were about 30 graduate students and 10 professors in the department. It behooved graduate students to socialize with the professors whose personal connections could translate into valuable professional advice, networks, and jobs. In the cluster of grad students, I recall eight women. When I first arrived at SU, there was one woman faculty member who would not receive tenure. Another woman filled this position.

Graduate school was a long initiation to a selective club. Classes were small and there were scholarly and social gatherings outside the department's walls at professors' homes; it was a version of community. Being on a first-name basis with professors was acceptable. One purpose of graduate school was to make us eventual colleagues to the people who were teaching us. At DB's invitation, I met him outside of class and he took me to dinner once or twice. We enjoyed discussing current events.

The biannual department retreats at Thornfield, a nearby conference center, were occasions when faculty and grad students mixed and
mingled over a day and a half of structured dialogue and shared meals.
Once, the grad students invaded (by invitation) the room of the newest
(and therefore youngest) professor and drank saki with him. We all felt
the effects the next morning. I am not sure of sleeping arrangements,
but, in "Downton Abbey" fashion, over the years, there were secret liaisons that occurred after "lights out." From many tales of these weekends,
a friend referred to Thornfield as "Hornfield."

There was a covert warning system among the women grad students about the men who held our futures in their hands, although this
knowledge didn't readily rise to the surface. The system failed when it
came to DB, as I received no warning about him. The women's system
kept inappropriate behavior known but forever under the radar. I was
naïve and shocked to find out that several women had had or were having affairs with professors. Although I understood that affairs usually
occurred between consenting adults, knowing they actively existed had
an impact on how I viewed the professionalism of the professor and the
participating woman.

Questions floated around about confirmed or suspected affairs. I feel
sure there was a lot that I did not know. I could discuss the situation with
my friend Cathie, also a student in the department. Would a professor be
able to distinguish the quality of his lover's work from that of other students? Was the obvious bond between the two giving the lover an edge?
How were we to behave toward the professor's spouse? We agreed that
these amorous situations made us most uncomfortable. They altered the
ground beneath us because we were not always aware of what was going
on. We learned that while women shared a secret alarm system about
men's behavior, the same women were content to have secret liaisons
with the same men. Both could be true.

Here's another member of the cast who disturbed me throughout
my time at SU: Dr. James Wiggins (JW), the director of graduate studies
in the Department of Religion. As his title implies, JW was an important
force for all graduate students. He offered graduate courses that most of

us took, and he guided our academic paths. His connections to the field of the study of religion were significant as graduate students completed their degrees and sought teaching positions at other universities.

The married JW was a notorious womanizer. I do not think his behavior was reported, although many observed it, as I did while attending retreat at Thornfield in 1976. . . .

JW leaned over the back of Amy's chair attentive. How can they both have so little pride? (JPS journal, April 2, 1976)

Early on, I was told that JW was having an affair with a married grad student (not the one referenced above).[30] Their bond was obvious in our seminar class, and it gave me anxiety to be around them. Somehow, I taught myself to navigate the obvious. When they broke up, I faced a peculiar situation because there were no etiquette rules to guide me. Now, the tension was of a different type that was harder to ignore. The best course of action turned out to be silence—condolences would have been awkward.

At a conference at Wellesley College in spring 1976, Linda, a former, rising star, graduate student who suddenly left the SU program in 1973 and never returned, greeted me. I knew her but not well, and I had wondered what had happened. She asked me, "How can you stand to be at Syracuse?" That was a good question. Linda told me that JW had arrived unannounced at her dorm door at 9 pm one evening and asked if he could come in. As a result, she left the program.

JW died in February 2017. One obituary described him as a philosopher, activist, and longtime professor of religion. Unlike DB, he was not approaching retirement in 1975 but was, instead, in the initial stages of rising to power in the department and in the field of religion studies. His national stature–he was head of the American Academy of Religion from 1983 to 1992–reflected brightly on the SU Department of Religion. His sexual affairs and harassment less so.

---

30 It could have been the "involved woman" who told me of the relationship/affair. She was in several of my courses.

We knew the culture was one of sexual harassment. Before we had a term for it, we knew it because we experienced it. We knew that what enveloped us was wrong because it was an obstacle in our paths to success.

From My Journal:

February 18, 1975—Just to add to the general confusion of my mind . . . at the end of my session with DB this afternoon, he said "May I say something personal?" I assented. He told me that he had dreamed about me on Sunday night and this prompted him to ask why I sometimes tried so hard to be unattractive without succeeding—was I afraid of dirty old men? Oh, Lordie, I don't know where to put this in my life. (1) Is he merely saying, I like you and want you to be happy the way others are? (2) Is he asking me why I don't wear skirts? (3) Is he making a pass at me so that I will never again feel comfortable in his presence? I try to understand, knowing he is a southern gentleman, perhaps he is paying me a compliment. I resent it however, not being able to imagine a woman professor taking aside a male grad student and saying to him "You would be so much more attractive if you wore bell-bottoms and combed your hair." He has violated my strict boundaries between academia and the rest of me—I incorporate the former, not vice versa. I walked down the hill slowly, close to tears, pissed off at this rap that I've heard before. My appearance is mine, not to be controlled by (man's) society's jurisdictions that a man wears pants and a woman shows her legs. I wonder whether I can trust him to be able to work with him. I thought of telling him of loving a woman, but knew he would not understand. Let's just hope this is all paternalistic.

In writing this piece, a memory returned. When I was the head resident advisor, I remember DB asking me—he was trying to be casual—which room was mine in Winchell dormitory? He captured the question inside an anecdote about waiting at the bus stop across the street from the dorm in the evening. "None of your business," I should have said but did not. After that, I kept my curtains drawn all the way, particularly in the evening. Fortunately, they were made of thick material and could keep out the cold as well as peeping Toms.

> *On March 29, 1975, at 1:15 AM—Professor DB Robertson called me, drunk on his ass, incoherent and rambling on about how I was the one person in the department that he loved the most. My heart beat faster and faster—there's nothing worse than a silly old fool. Except I resent having to handle it at all. He put me here. Talk to Cavanagh? I think I could, he's compassionate, he would listen. Talk to DB? But anything I might say to him he might take as encouragement. Sleeping through the night sounds like the best idea.* (JPS journal). Recorded in my memory is that DB said he loved me because I read The New York Times.

> *March 30, 1975—But tomorrow I have resolved to speak with RC about DB. . . . This man has really sewed up things well. I fully believe that it will be impossible for me to work with him—I will always remember this. I am not too coherent, but a journal permits and accepts any level of incoherence which you might want to present to it. I am so tired. . . .*

I brought my parents into the situation on our weekly Sunday telephone call. I recorded this painful comment:

> *March 30, 1975—Mother said in jest this morning after I told them about DB, "Well, now we'll just have to marry you off." But there is <u>no</u> solution in that. And I said as much. . . .*

This "humorous" comment aside, my parents did their best to be supportive, and they worried for my career aspirations. They discussed the situation with my lawyer sister. They came for a visit in May 1975, and I took them to the department to meet various people and to see where I spent a lot of time. As was his usual practice, DB was there, and he struck up a conversation with my ever-congenial father and my father engaged. Mother and I stood in the hallway by the elevator looking at both of them—they were about 20 feet away—and despite both nonverbal and verbal signals that we transmitted down the corridor, my father continued to talk with DB. He seemed to enjoy himself but I felt fully betrayed, even as I understood my father would always choose nonconfrontation.

Long distance but vital support came via international mail from my girlfriend Lynne, who wrote to me from Spain (April 3, 1975) where she was studying for a semester.

> *And DB—I actually considered sending him your quotes attached to a note—explaining I was a (friend or lover I haven't decided) probably friend to be safe—who had received your dilemma—your inquiries as to what do I do? And if he could see your position without you having to embarrass both of you (JPS & DB) by cooling or screaming or quitting he might once again act like the man you (JPS) respected instead of some pathetic old man.—I don't know him—or he me—it matters not, and I WANT THAT MAN TO KNOCK IT OFF WITHOUT KNOCKING YOU UP, AROUND OR DOWN. Babe, sweet woman I love, I refrain until I hear from you. I will not enter your affairs unless asked. But it's an option—as is having your dad talk to him as 2 men old enough to be your father.*

In my journal I described my meeting with RC and my emotions leading up to a meeting with RC and DB.

> *March 31, 1975—At 12 noon sharp, I entered the confines of RC's office and began to tell my story. He listened without interruption and when it was his turn to speak began by apologizing for DB and told me that no student should have to take what I've put up with. He was compassionate, dignified, and also offended. W/o my suggesting it, he said that he would confront DB. Appar-*

*ently, it is not the first time he's [DB] made calls in the wee hours
of the morning. The proof of all this—DB's absence this morning
(1ˢᵗ morning he's missed in weeks!). And RC managed to help me
by explaining that he could understand DB's attraction to my personality, he himself felt me to be warm and open and at Thornfield had felt no reticence about coming up to me and speaking
with me as I sat on a bench looking at Lake Cazenovia. What
he said to me was a very human statement, which I greatly appreciated. Further, he understood how I had responded to DB
and why I had so responded, understood my hurt, my anger,
my worries about the thesis and my future. It seems that he be-
lieves that the Graduate Committee would be willing to waive
certain restrictions and permit me to go outside the Department
to American Studies to find a thesis adviser. I do not envy RC's
impending conversation—an alcoholic can frequently be a mar-
tyr—nor do I await my impending confrontation with DB.
He will no doubt push for a tête-à-tête, but it might be easier to
incur his wrath than a conversation where he apologized, beat
his breast, shed a few tears, in short, a Thornfield production.*
[After dinner at Thornfield was the time for skits, jokes, and
drinking.]

April Fool's Day 1975—*Obviously, no one in the department has ever faced up to the facts of his [DB's] alcoholism, cov-
ering up nicely for him even when he took a taxi ride for $160 to
Minnowbrook [an SU conference center located 135 miles from
Syracuse] last spring. And if no one else has ever faced up to it,
there is no reason and/or need for him to do so.*

April 5, 1975, 12:30 AM—*Butterflies which feel more
like lethal moths in my tummy—sometime next week, a meeting
between DB, RC, and myself. DB denies a sexual advance, he has
been impotent for 20 years. What could I be thinking about? (I
fear the telephone and its ring.) He wanted only to bring me out*

of my <u>reserved</u> nature. Of course, he had 4 days to think up his an-
swers. It will take all my strength to meet this confrontation—no
tears there. I tried to imagine it and succeeded all too well, which
makes my stomach begin to churn all the more.

*   **April 9, 1975**—Show me the man who understands/no*
just concedes/the existence of the continued <u>sexual</u> assault against
women conducted by men. Time heals and my memories of this
will also fade, but some part of me will remember enough to make
me wonder every time there is a remote chance, every time there is
ambiguity, oh yes. Thank you, Dr. Robertson.

*   **April 22, 1975**—I worry about my work for DB, knowing*
that the pressure is upon me to produce a very good piece of work,
but I have not done much for him in the past 4-5 weeks and feel
even less inclined now to plug away at any material for him. My
being a scholar has nothing to do with him yet I feel more motivat-
ed when working for someone I respect and like.

My journal does not include a description of the meeting with DB
and RC. I resort to my memory.

We were together for 15 minutes, which felt like a very long time.
RC's office was small with windows on one side that looked south to
the courtyard. I cannot remember what time of day, but perhaps late
morning or early afternoon as sunlight (an extraordinary occurrence in
perpetually cloudy Syracuse) was streaming in. RC sat behind his desk,
which was perpendicular to the window. There was a bookcase behind
him. DB sat by the window and I by the door, which was shut. DB's and
my chairs were close together—we could have touched each other with
little effort. I was shaky and emotional and was trying hard to control
my demeanor—it was creepy to be so close to him. My voice might have
wavered a bit but my anger strongly fortified me and prevented me from
crying. I recounted everything that had happened—enumerating all the
odd encounters from the first at the bus stop, to unasked-for-person-

al remarks, to the late-night phone call. DB denied everything. At one point he thundered, "I don't know what she's talking about. I've been impotent for 20 years." But he also blamed his conduct on medication that he was taking. I took these statements as the closest he would ever come to an admission of his behavior.

Close enough to touch,
my story disclosed actions
of the man next to me.
(Haiku, JPS 2018)

☾   ☾   ☾

I give credit to RC for listening to my complaint, taking it seriously, and acting quickly in the short term. If university policy addressed this type of situation, it could only have been in the vaguest of terms. RC's suggestion of a shared session with DB certainly seems appropriate to the era and to an academic setting relying on discourse to air different perspectives. Perhaps, RC hoped we could work things out without too much drama. I did not expect that the meeting would devolve into an embarrassing situation of "she said, he said," which it did. Maybe RC didn't anticipate that either. I entered my threesome with DB and RC thinking that there would be a resolution. There was a degree of justice meted out but it was not satisfying.

As I had requested, RC disentangled my studies from DB. He agreed that I did not have to attend any more classes with him, and I fulfilled course requirements through independent study. There was no discussion of DB becoming my dissertation adviser. I did not receive a written report of the meeting.

I cringe when revisiting my journal entry for March 31, 1975. RC's statement to me about my personality seems at best quaint and at worst inappropriate. I'm not sure how my personality (however my professors characterized it) became a topic of discussion and I'm not sure why I accepted that as okay, as in this example: *What he said to me was a very hu-*

man statement which I greatly appreciated. I presume I was grateful for some affirmation and sympathy. RC's empathy and concrete response probably made the difference for me in deciding not to pursue my complaint to higher levels, although I did not realize that there were other options within the system. In 1975, I was on my own to understand what had happened. Now, supposedly, women are taken at their word.

My experience was different, not opposite, per se. Of significance, mine featured a less-receptive audience. I told my story to the administrative powers, other students, friends, professors, family, and acquaintances, and I received an empathetic but passive response that, nevertheless, helped to steady me as I confronted DB. Not a single person suggested I should rock the boat any more than I already had, although Lynne came the closest. No one was affected by my palpable rage.

In this age, which I hesitate to consider significantly more enlightened, there are many more resources about sexual harassment and abuse. Molly Roberts offers an observation to chew on:

> *The struggle of a woman who levels an allegation against one of these men is so great because, in reality, she is never challenging one man. She is challenging the clique and the culture he belongs to—his high school, his college, his country club, his political party or his industry.* [31]

As applied to my case, my complaint challenged the solidarity of the small, overwhelmingly male faculty. If DB had been forced to resign in the face of my complaint, the department might have lost one of its tenured positions. Faculty members knew about DB's teaching while drunk, and their silence on the topic implied tolerance, and that suggests the department enabled him. He possessed significant power as a tenured professor. For the department, I believe it was more difficult and worrisome to unseat him and lose funding for his position

---

31 washingtonpost.com/blogs/post-partisan, *The Washington Post,* September 26, 2018. Molly Roberts commenting on the nomination of Brett Kavanaugh to the US Supreme Court. Roberts is an editor, writer, and producer for *The Washington Post's* Opinion section.

than to confront the issues that he brought to the department's culture.

I want the Department of Religion to know that there is history between the department and me. It would not bother me one bit if my letter of October 8, 2018, caused a small flurry of anxiety; indeed, I would find that satisfying.

It is relatively easy to summarize the details of my encounter with DB. It is harder to describe the invisible scaffolding actively supporting DB's behavior. My journal from this period offers more examples of the male culture that surrounded me. The department was never a comfortable or safe space for me, although to some degree, I blamed myself for my awkwardness.

As the graduate student representative, I accepted an invitation to a faculty meeting on June 18, 1976.

> *I felt much uneasiness about going into the room—Crossing the Line—and once inside and sitting next to Dan [my professor friend], I felt no better. DB and JW manned the other side of the table. DB is so pathetic, if he were 10 years younger, I'd call him an ass hole. JW spent the half hour staring at me—my Paranoia I wondered?—but I stared at my crotch. I want to tell him that there is no mystery about my body, it's a woman's body with 2 breasts, brownish pubic hair surrounding my sex. It's mine, ah, Jesus, he's just an* ass! *I thought about Amanda [the department's newest faculty hire] having to sit here every week—does RC introduce her as 'a young lady?' The analogy to entering a man's fraternity was apt, but . . . I don't wonder about what it does to them—there are* more *of them and always will be—but I worry I can't handle it. It should be that way wherever I go.*
> (JPS journal, June 18, 1976)

Of another trip to a department conference at Thornfield on September 27, 1976, I described a scenario with popular and rising faculty star, David Miller (DM). He sat:

> *... at the table talking about phallic symbols while he licked and stroked a cigar. Since the previous evening, I had resisted the interpretation being given—the talk of heroes made me suspicious, but by the time DM told about learning to kiss from a woman (still persisting in his masculine language, the woman <u>penetrated his</u> mouth) I was angry. Ah, he told me, 'Don't think that the sword is just a penis, it has a feminine side to it, the Medusa.' But who slew the Medusa?[32] We broke, I was angry still, and wrote down my question. ... JW emulates DM, does he think him the masculine epitome? ... [after the break] They called for audience participation, my hand shot up. Tentatively, I began but gathered force in my question. I felt good. 'In two days why has no one mentioned that the pen is mightier than the sword?'*

Most graduate students admired DM—he was especially adept at speaking, magically mesmerizing his audience as he wrapped up his topic in one word. It was impressive, particularly the first time one was captive to his performance. DM was not my favorite but I admired his facility and knowledge. Of the same occasion, I wrote:

> *Later finding his phallic symbols upon the conference table [these were actual objects] when I was running the grad student meeting; I contemplated a mimicry of his act in the lighting of a cigar.* (JPS journal, September 27, 1976)

Returning to Molly Roberts:

> *A woman is never challenging only one in-group, either. She is challenging the culture of the whole country, where power feeds on power and once a man has won enough, it is unlikely anyone will let him lose.[33]*

---

32 Perseus, who then used Medusa's head as a weapon to turn other people to stone. Perseus was the son of Zeus and the mortal Danaë.
33 Roberts, Ibid.

Thus, the patriarchy protected these men and, I assume, others. It has to do so because it cannot operate otherwise.

As far as I know, there were no repercussions to DB for his behavior. He kept on keeping on until his retirement. JW, by most professional and academic measurements, and despite his sexual harassment and indiscretions, had a successful career.

There were repercussions for me, however.

> *Water drips on stone —*
> *sexual harassment's toll*
> *erodes over time.*
> (Haiku, JPS 2018)

☾　　☾　　☾

Emotional repercussions were subtle, but they manifested in loneliness, dissatisfaction with my studies, and an intensified whittling away of my recently acquired self-confidence. And there was this striking journal entry:

> *But it's not surprising that I'm worked up. This mess with DB has brought such a combination of fear, hardness, coldness and contempt inside me that I search hard in my memory to remember ever feeling this way before.* (JPS journal, April 5, 1975)

The DB/Jill story could read as merely an unfortunate incident. We can all attest to awkwardness in personal relationships, not excluding our most intimate of intimates. Cultural and organizational mores were different in the 1970s. My choice to testify to my experience was unusual because women rarely risked reporting sexual harassment; they were too busy trying to manage it.

Maybe DB misinterpreted our friendly exchanges. Maybe he had not dealt with women as professionals or women who were becoming professionals. His southern ways were his manner.

I was never in any physical danger from him. He was frail, maybe 69 and his years of drinking had taken a physical toll. After his harassment, I saw him as disgusting and pathetic.

In department life, it was impossible to predict when I would run into the social butterfly who was DB, encounters that were always uncomfortable and stressful. I became adept at ignoring him in the department office and hallways and in engineering my path away from him at a party. It was a long time before I felt calm answering my phone in my dorm apartment.

I have no proof that I was explicitly branded a pariah within the department, but over time, I felt that professors and some student colleagues saw me as a troublemaker or radioactive student—someone to treat carefully. I discerned the emotional difference between inclusion and exclusion. In the grad student group, I had been vocal about the need for the department to support our efforts in finding teaching jobs. After I moved away and was working full time, I had a dispute about my commitment to my thesis with my new dissertation advisor (a woman) and ended up changing advisers midstream. Again, I was yet another trouble for the department.

The intensity of my journal entries and my memories of this time reinforce the devastating nature and difficulty I had in confronting this incident. DB's harassment came from left field and shook up my academic plans while I was coming out as Lesbian. It was a chaotic, emotional time. There was something egregious happening in the department. The department had a DB problem and it also had a major departmental problem of a thriving culture of sexual harassment. DB's behavior was chronic and reprehensible but he was not the sole actor. The department's inaction was not acceptable.

I have had many creepy encounters with men that I squirreled away, such as unwanted sexual invitations from older men when I was a child, near misses on the sexual assault front, too-frequent incidents of men touching me on public transportation, construction workers and random men calling out slurs, men following me in cars as I walked on city streets, the too-many publicly masturbating men I have encountered in various cities, my first date in college with a man who made it hard for me to return to my dorm, and the vice president of a trade association who lewdly complimented me on my breasts at an office farewell party for a colleague. Also, there were the men who thought themselves appealing when they inquired about my attire, implying that I was hiding my body.

My experiences do not differ from that of many women. We survive these completely distasteful things, and we rarely talk about them. What would be the point? They are icky. Even in the company of women, we might not find the succor we need.

> *Women have always lied to each other. Women have always whispered the truth to each other. Both of these axioms are true.*[34]

Reading my journal, I celebrate with strong pride how I handled DB. I sought advice and support. I confronted him and I survived the experience, having made my own decision about the path I would take. Looking back, I am amazed that I spoke out and only regret that my pride was not strong enough to carry the fight further. However, these repercussions ended my long-held aspiration to become a university professor. During college, I was eager for the academic dialogue that occurred inside and outside class. I loved studying and reading. I came to think of teaching at the college level as my ideal career path.

Post-DB, I never felt fully supported by my department. I came to doubt my abilities vis-à-vis teaching, research, and writing. I harbor a modicum of doubt still. There is a part of me that feels that my PhD was given rather than awarded in full recognition of my work.

All tenure-track positions in my field were already filled by someone my age shortly before I received my PhD, which made my aspirations seem far-fetched and probably hopeless. I wondered and worried about what kind of reference I could expect from the department—would word of my "personality" travel to other universities? Ours was a small

---

34 Adrienne Rich. These notes were first read at the Hartwick Writers' Workshop, Oneonta, NY, June 1975.

world and people were likely to know each other and could read between the lines of reference letters.[35]

These factors contributed to my departure in 1977 from Syracuse to Washington, DC, and a delay in completing my dissertation. I found much satisfaction in my career choices. University life remains appealing but I realize that teaching, research, and writing are rewarded outside the halls of academe.

No doubt sexual harassment continued for me and no doubt it continues for many women. Sexual harassment is tightly knit into the structural discrimination prominent in our government, corporations, other organizations, and family life. No doubt my career path changed. No doubt I regretted the loss of my imagined teaching career. No doubt this experience made me angry and fueled my activism. Politics of any kind became personal. No doubt. No doubt.

For the first time, as I write, it occurs to me I might have been played. The Department of Religion knew exactly what it was doing as it handled my complaint to "resolution." Perhaps they meant to keep me swimming in the same unhealthy waters until I completed my PhD. Maybe I was to pay for the discomfort I caused. I doubt I will ever know.

My framed diploma remains in my closet. I think that's the best place for it.

APPENDIX

At the suggestion of two friends with connections to SU, I sent a second letter bypassing the Department of Religion.

October 4, 2019
Mr. Kent Syverud
Chancellor and President
Syracuse University

---

35 Six women students filed *Alexander vs. Yale* in 1980, alleging sexual harassment from Yale University professors and administrators. Although the case was not decided in the students' favor, they achieved their objectives: Yale instituted a grievance procedure and the court held that sexual harassment constituted sex discrimination.

900 South Crouse Avenue
Syracuse, NY 13244

Dear Chancellor Syverud:
Almost a year ago, I sent the enclosed letter to Dr. Philip P.
Arnold, Chair, Department of Religion at Syracuse University. I
have never received a response.

Because of your personal concern for addressing sexual and
relationship violence on the university campus, I believe you would
be interested in my experience, albeit in 1974-1977 when I resided
in Syracuse as a graduate student.

I repeat my request from my letter to Dr. Arnold–that this
incident be recorded in the history of the Department of Religion
and the University. I would appreciate acknowledgement of re-
ceipt of this letter and description of any action taken as a result.
Thank you.
Sincerely,
Jill P. Strachan, PhD
Washington, D.C.

Responses arrived shortly thereafter. First, came the lawyers.

VIA FEDERAL EXPRESS (OVERNIGHT)

October 30, 2019
Jill P. Strachan
Washington, D.C.
RE: Letters dated October 25, 2018 and October 4, 2019

Dear Dr. Strachan:
Syracuse University is in receipt of the enclosed letters dated Oc-
tober 25, 2018 and October 4, 2019, which were referred to our office
for a response. Thank you for bringing this matter to our attention.
The University prohibits harassment related to any protected

category including, without limitation, race, color, creed, religion, national origin, citizenship, ethnicity, marital status, age, disability, sexual orientation, gender identity and gender expression, veteran status, or any other status protected by applicable law. We take all allegations seriously. Our office will meet with the Dean of Arts & Sciences to ensure your letter is properly reviewed and recorded.

In the meantime, if you have questions or concerns please do not hesitate to reach out.

Very truly yours,
Gabriel Nugent
Deputy General Counsel
Office of University Counsel
Followed by this letter:

Friday, November 15, 2019

Dear Dr. Strachan,

Thank you so much for your letter. I apologize for the lack of response from the department chair to your recent letter, and will ensure that your letter be recorded in the permanent history of the department.

I am very sorry to hear about your experiences, and of others. I am especially troubled to hear about the mechanism, which was chosen to address the issue, including a meeting with the chair, Professor Robertson and yourself. I can only imagine the stress this must have caused you.

Many years later, I am happy to report that processes are in place that allow for independent investigations, through our Title IX office, as well as robust procedures to deal with violations against the University's harassment policies.

Again, thank you for bringing this to my attention. My deepest apologies to the earlier lack of response. I will ensure that your letter be retained in the permanent archives.

With warm regards,
Karin Ruhlandt

Dean, Distinguished Professor of Chemistry
College of Arts and Sciences
cc: Philip Arnold, Chair Religion Department
December 5, 2019

Dr. Karin Ruhlandt
Dean, Distinguished Professor of Chemistry
College of Arts & Sciences
Syracuse University
203 Tolley Humanities Building
Syracuse, NY 13244

Dear Dean Ruhlandt:
Thank you for your letter of November 15, 2019 in which you ensured me that my letters of October 25, 2018 to Dr. Philip Arnold, Chair Religion Department, and October 4, 2019 to Chancellor Kent Syverud have been retained in Syracuse University's permanent archives.

Thank you for helping me to be counted. You can likely understand how important it is to me that my voice has been recognized. I am most appreciative of your interest in what happened.

It is gratifying to read that the University has addressed the need for independent investigations of sexual harassment through its Title IX office. I wouldn't wish on anyone anything similar to what I experienced, but, I recognize, that the times were different.

If the College of Arts & Sciences should ever hold a conference, colloquium, and/or workshop about sexual harassment, I would be interested in speaking about my experience. In addition, I have written an essay about what happened to me. If there is any possibility of publication of this piece through Syracuse University, I would be interested in pursuing such an opportunity.

Again, thank you for your letter. It was well-received.
Sincerely,
Jill P. Strachan
Washington, D.C.

YOU HAVE NO ENEMIES,
ONLY FRIENDS

A LONG-DISTANCE phone call with my mother was always brief because she was concerned about extravagance and still, well into the 1970s, a little bit suspicious of technology. On a weekly call in the spring of 1976, with her in Washington, DC, and me in Syracuse, New York, she described how a few days before she had been robbed on 14th Street NW as she waited at a bus stop. A young man grabbed her small change purse from her hand. It held her bus fare and car keys. My mother, at 69, chased him and easily caught up to him. He stopped running, calculating perhaps that an older woman would never contemplate chasing him much less catch up to him. "Young man, give me back my purse," she demanded. He did not respond. She repeated her request, and he flung the purse in her face and ran off. She returned to the bus stop in time to catch the next bus home. Despite my concerned exclamations and questions, Mother did not particularly express any emotion about what had happened, and she soon hung up. As always, she was keeping tabs in her mind on the long-distance costs.

Until my mid-twenties, I unreservedly preferred my father.

*I miss Daddy a lot. I think I love him more than Mother
because he stands up for me.* (JPS diary, August 1, 1961)

My mother, Evelyn Berglund Strachan, was intrepid, always unfail-
ingly polite, and, yes, a bit stubborn. These characteristics shaped my
mother's unusual life, making her bold and transforming her into a
woman who forged past obstacles propped up by others. She had strongly held beliefs that she expressed freely. At her civil marriage, she refused
to say she would "obey" her husband. One of her dearly held convictions was that women had the short end of the stick. She volunteered for
Planned Parenthood (located near the bus stop on 14th Street NW) and
various women's groups that were fueled by mission rather than catering
to the demands of social advancement and social status.

She followed national and international news and did not balk at stating her opinions in the company of diplomats and academics. She decried
the commercialism of holidays such as Valentine's Day, Mother's Day, and
Father's Day. I remember her telling me, "Every day is Mother's Day."

☾   ☾   ☾

Mother loved roses, ate lettuce like she was a rabbit, and eschewed over-
head lighting. She enjoyed museums, where she carefully examined each exhibit from beginning to end and read every caption. She kept the household
accounts in ledger books and was our family's most dedicated saver. She was
mistress of our collective household, which included our various dogs from
Greece, Egypt, and Sri Lanka, all of whom were her loving companions.

In all her life preparing food for family and guests, she never once
cooked more food than she deemed necessary. As a person who could
make a single Hershey chocolate bar last for several weeks, she believed
that big portions bordered on moral failure. I asked her once if an act of
exuberance had ever caused her to overeat anything. She replied that she
had once eaten a pound of Bing cherries when she was pregnant with
my sister Heather. The experience was never repeated, or so I gathered.

In one of my earliest memories when I was younger than five, I sit on the inside basement steps of our suburban Virginia rental house watching her iron in dim light. Sensing a strand of hair on her shoulder, Mother reaches up with her hand to move it back. She does this several times without success. Eventually, I realize that she is batting back the tail of a dead rat lying on the beam above her. My face conveys my alarm to her because I do not have words for what I am seeing. Mother looks up and then back at me. She quietly asks me to go upstairs, which I do.

This same calm spirit prevailed in other circumstances that include hordes of cockroaches swiftly swarming out of cracks onto kitchen counters, engine troubles far from gas stations, and unwanted men approaching her. Once, in Cairo, the *suffragi* (the Egyptian word for a household cook and bearer) lifted his caftan to show her his "wares." She did not wait for her husband to return from work. She fired him immediately. I have never been so brave.

Given her Germanic and Finnish roots, Mother might have had a serious countenance, but laughter was intrinsic to her conversation. She enjoyed puns and they occurred to her frequently. A pun did not have to be good, especially if it was her own. When she thought of one, she would laugh so hard that she appeared to be choking. Her often-repeated and favorite pun referred to meeting Alan, her future husband and my father, on a tennis court. In her parlance, "It was a love match."

Mother enjoying a joke (most likely a pun), c. 1952

Her generosity of spirit was revealed by her impeccable manners and her many friendships, her engagement with her daughters' friends, and by the various visitors who graced the family table all year long, not just for Thanksgiving and Christmas meals. She was empathetic and always quick with a kind gesture. When living in southwest Washington, DC, she took daily walks "helllooooing" and smiling to all she encountered. The sullen and the exuberant alike received her kind greetings, including Hubert H. Humphrey, who lived nearby.

She hoped for, modeled, and supported better times for her two daughters as women, envisioning us as successful professionals with happy families. She believed education was key and she made personal sacrifices to pay for our ballet and music lessons. Before Heather went to college, Mother made a lot of her clothes and used the leftover material to make mine. Many years later, she confessed that she hated sewing.

Mother was an avid correspondent with family and friends. She kept a carbon copy of her outgoing letters on exceedingly thin onion skin paper. This carbon copy was stapled to the letter to which she was responding and then filed. She sent handwritten notes to acknowledge birthdays and deaths. She maintained household accounts and wrote related business letters, signing them "(Mrs.) Evelyn B. Strachan." The "B" stood for Berglund, her maiden name. Berglund was an American adaptation of a Finnish surname, Bjorkbakka (she told me it meant "birch tree"), which became Bjorklund and then Berglund in its own journey.

She started keeping a nearly daily diary on January 1, 1933, and kept pace with it until 1988. Here is her first entry, written when she lived in Detroit.

> *This diary is the gift of a unique creature, and may I say platitudinously would were I worthy of such a friend. After seeing Murray Hill at the Bonstelle with the Toddlers, Alan and I spent the rest of the evening (N.Y.'s Eve) alone, playing all of the 5 records and _____ . Wrote minutes, dinner at home.*

I assume she was referring to her role as secretary to Detroit's Branch One Socialist Party, which was the largest in the Michigan Socialist Party.

I think her drawing of a blank line was to conceal their post dinner activities. On Daddy's 76th birthday, she acknowledged the special place that December 31, 1932, held for them.

> *On a new Year's Eve*
> *Yes, eons ago*
> *when Time was young*
> *Didst though foresee...*

My parents married in September 1933, after dating for a couple of years as they waited without success for the Depression to end. I surmise that a combination of a medical condition for Mother and the practice of birth control delayed my sister's birth until 1940.

In 1926, when she was 19, Mother left the small, sleepy world of Manistee, Michigan, her hometown, for business school in St. Paul.[36] Her father Matt Berglund did not have a vision for his only daughter beyond the socially accepted path, although he came to rely on her, particularly after his wife Freida Schultz Berglund (her mother) died, leaving a teenage son still at home. An immigrant from Finland, my grandfather arrived in the US at the age of seven. After my parents married, it took him a decade to come to terms with Mother's marriage to a naturalized Englishman. Despite his naturalization as a US citizen, my grandfather did not consider his son-in-law to be American enough, although he came to enjoy his company. Struggling with her father's odd and conservative opinions strengthened my mother's sense of justice and provided practice for articulating her point of view in a bigger world and in discussions with her husband.

One of Grandfather's jobs was as a lifeguard on Lake Michigan. He taught his sons to swim but not his daughter, because he believed she would never need to know. He expected her to learn the duties of motherhood and to execute them. Once when Freida, my grandmother, traveled by train to a funeral in California, Mother took over all the house-

---

36 In 1900, Manistee was home to 22,700 people. However, as the century progressed, the city's population dropped to around 8,000 people, and is currently listed at 6,226 per 2010 census. Source: Wikipedia.

hold duties for several weeks, including cooking dinner for him and, at the time, her two brothers. He did not help at all. When a neighbor banged on the door during dinner one evening to say that grandfather's 'roof was on fire, he responded "Let it burn!" It was left to my mother to resolve the situation.

I heard this story many times in my life, thinking it was funny, and only recently began to wonder whether he was drinking, and whether he was an alcoholic. Mother never said. My grandfather considered himself to be more American than my naturalized father and he expressed in person and in letters his suspicions of "Negroes" and Polish immigrants, many of whom, like his own people, the Finns, came to Michigan in the early 1900s.

My grandfather was insistent that he be buried in a cement coffin because he did not want bugs and worms getting him. Mother tried to change his mind but he won in the end, as she was living in Greece when he died. He got the coffin he wanted.

> *Detroit, Michigan, April 1947*
> *Monday evening I was more then shocked to learn the news about Alan's job. I thought he had a life's leash on that job. I know Alan will land some thing as good or better.*
> *I am enclosing you a check $35.00. I want you use $5.00 on your self. I was going to buy a slip but I did not know your sice [size] will you tel me what you bought. I wanted you to have that five dollars for your birth as I know it is on ___ this month. . . . I wish you many more happy birthdays and trust Allan have landed something. . . . A good honest American is entitled to good living. Well Evelyn if you should need any assistance your dad will stick with you to my last dollar. I am your dad M.B.*

She honed her political views through active membership in the Socialist Party of America led by Norman Thomas. Both she and Daddy met different, interesting people in that milieu, and they always acknowledged the positive impacts of the Socialist Party in their lives. They became staunch Democrats, voted for FDR four times, and for every Democratic presidential candidate thereafter. Mother was a direct benefactress of the Nineteenth Amendment to the US Constitution, which gave white, American women the right to vote. She was 13 on August 18, 1920, when it was ratified and she never missed the opportunity to exercise her vote, even when she lived overseas.

Along with two friends, Louise McCoy and Doris Foster, Evelyn (now 71) marched for the extension of the Equal Rights Amendment[37] on July 9, 1978. It was a blazing, humid day in Washington, DC, long before water in plastic bottles became readily available. The three of them joyously walked at the front of the march, joining 100,000 women dressed in white who filled the national Mall and the steps of the US Capitol. I was there as well, marching at the tail end.

Mother, with her business education, had much more schooling than Daddy, who left school permanently at 14, and his eventual success as a diplomat was due to Mother's tutelage and his willingness to improve. She corrected his spoken and written grammar and reviewed what he wrote. In the 1930s, in Detroit, she took classes to become a social worker. She worked until she became pregnant with my sister Heather. Labor practices would have allowed her employer to fire her because of her pregnancy. She did not complete a formal degree.

As a diplomat's wife, Mother was part of a team, albeit not one officially recognized by the US Department of State. She and her children were "dependents," a term she despised because it implied she was an appendage. In the early days of my father's career, the US Foreign Service (USFS) evaluated the unpaid wife along with the husband. A wife could either enhance her husband's career or bring it down. Children's behavior on post was part of the calculation of career success.

Public recognitions of women, even by their husbands, were limited and often delivered in a humorous and slightly condescending manner. This style maintained the social order of man's place and work. He was

---

37 The Equal Rights Amendment is a proposed amendment to the United States Constitution designed to guarantee equal legal rights for all American citizens regardless of sex. It seeks to end the legal distinctions between men and women in matters of divorce, property, employment, and other matters. Source: Wikipedia.

in charge, even when he relied upon the assistance of women. Here is a notable example.

When President Kennedy (JFK) and First Lady Jackie Kennedy traveled to Paris in June 1961, the French were completely taken with the First Lady, and she was the overwhelming focus of press coverage. The situation prompted JFK to remark to the press:

> *I do not think it altogether inappropriate to introduce myself.*
> *I am the man who accompanied Jacqueline Kennedy to Paris.*

Of course, I laugh at his wit, who could not? But take a moment to think why JFK's comment was even necessary. Its only purpose was to reestablish his superior position over a woman.

As the family linguist, Mother studied Urdu in Pakistan and Arabic and French in Cairo. With a practical knowledge of German (from her mother) and Greek (from a posting in Greece), she called herself a "kitchen" linguist because her vocabulary related to activities carried out in the kitchen. Mother used English and Arabic to plan meals with the cook who did our shopping in the local market in Cairo. Egyptians do not distinguish between consonants "b" and "p," so Mother would request peas and to her puzzlement, the cook always purchased beans. I did not mind because I preferred beans. She resolved the situation by drawing a pea (she had taken several art lessons) and by learning the correct Arabic word for peas, *bazila*.

Her last diary entries date from July and August 1988, when she and Daddy visited Greece and England. (These postretirement trips began in 1973 and ended in 1991.) They rented their usual, modest apartment on the island of Naxos for the month of July. Mother was 81 and Daddy was about to turn 85.

While in Naxos in 1988, Mother fell and broke her left wrist. She could not get medical treatment there and waited several days before she consulted a doctor in Athens. She relates these details matter-of-factly without mentioning pain or discomfort. She also discovered she had broken two fingers. It is not surprising that her handwriting in her diary suffered but she continued to chronicle events meticulously.

After Naxos, it was on to London to see the special exhibits of Picasso and Cezanne in the museums as well as concerts by the Scottish Symphony Orchestra, and plays such as "*Driving Miss Daisy*" and "*Letice and Lovage*" while visiting old friends and a few remaining relatives from my father's side of the family. Of the Picasso exhibit at the Tate Gallery, Mother noted:

> *... the very early but extremely sexy paintings. .... I wonder how long they will draw crowds. Certainly not our favorites.*
> (August 6, 1988)

A week's tour on a canal barge was also part of the fun.

> *We walked a good mile, with lock changes until late morn. We came aboard because of lack of a good path. After lunch I must have slept for 2 hours. About 4:30 after tea, we went out to explore the town as we had passed such a beautiful park. But trains go at about 100-miles per hour thru this town of Berkhamsted. There are remains of a 12th cent. Castle here of King William I. But those who did see it said it is a shambles. There were 2 women visitors at dinner, previous tour park clients. Very warm today, yes hot.* (August 14, 1988)

Mother was not favorably disposed to anyone's own self-approval. Around my fifth year, I asked her, *Mother, do you think I'm pretty?* To which she replied, *To me, you are.* Then, she followed up with a compliment, *You have very straight toes.*

She could project her voice over a significant distance, particularly in a department store. When accompanying her, I had license to roam but the moment would come when she would call my name in her "department store voice." No matter where I ventured, even to another floor, I could hear her. If I ignored her voice, it only became louder and more penetrating. I was sure that everyone could hear her and knew that I was the object of her search. My acute embarrassment could only be mitigated by appearing in person.

For style, Mother was a natural at presentation of her clothing and her home. At her most casual, she was beautifully stylish; she rarely wore slacks or shorts; T-shirts were unknown. Her costume jewelry, much of it purchased in Greece, was tasteful and matched her wardrobe. She could have easily modeled clothing for older women with her 5'7" frame and thin physique, complemented by her vibrantly colored outfits. She could not have walked the runway, however, because one hip was significantly higher than the other, which made her walk on a diagonal. Daddy called her distinctive gait a "sailor's walk." Mother took it as a tease, or I should say, she took it in stride but I think now that his comment bordered on being unkind.

Clearing her closet after she and Daddy unwillingly moved to a nursing home in Culpeper, Virginia, in 1993, I discovered that her clothes—from sweaters to evening wear and in between—looked almost new. Some items, like her cashmere sweaters, were over 40 years old and in flawless condition. Her dress shoes and regular shoes looked only slightly worn. It was obvious that she took exceedingly good care of what she owned.

As a little girl, I would sit on a small chair by her dressing table and watch her get ready for the day. She did not fuss at all but kept her toilette simple—a pale or sometimes light red lipstick, a bit of eyebrow pencil, and a brush of blush (although it was face powder then). Her naturally blond hair kept much of its color into her early eighties. She had regular appointments at the beauty parlor for a wash and set, and she kept her hair simply brushed away from her face.

She carefully selected everything from her jewelry to table settings to pieces of art. In each country where she lived, she selected crafts and art that have stood the test of time. Her eye distinguished the most interesting, novel paintings. Without formal training in the visual arts, she took time to research contemporary artists and sometimes befriended them.

Mother's purchase of a small, bronze statue of the Hindu elephant god Ganesha (God of wisdom, success, and good luck) resulted in a friendship with renowned Sri Lankan sculptor Tissa Ranasinghe and his wife Sally. When Tissa, Sally, and their two children moved to London, my parents reconnected with them annually. When I made a surprise visit to London for Daddy's 85th birthday in August 1988, Tissa and Sally took us to their favorite Sri Lankan restaurant. During our excellent meal, our young server recognized Tissa, and they celebrated that they came from the same village, Yogiyana, where Tissa was born in 1925. When Daddy died in November 1996, Tissa wrote to Heather and me.

Sally and I were saddened by the news of Alan's death. Please know we share your grief. We looked forward to their annual London visits—we met to have a meal together and I accompanied both to galleries and museums. Evelyn's 'Strachan-o-Log' was worth waiting for. They are the 'Good Americans' and good human beings. . . . It has been our privilege to have known them. Evelyn never failed to bring presents to the children. . . .

Unlike some daughters, I am not compelled to reminisce about Mother's cooking except to say that her spaghetti sauce, which contained celery as an extender, was something that she cooked for sizeable groups of people. They liked it better than I did.

Ironically, for one who shunned sweets, Mother made a memorable sour cherry pie. I have only rarely tasted pie that called to mind what she created. Its origin and recipe are lost; perhaps it was handed down from her mother. There are a lot of cherries in Michigan.

When I come across her red, metal pastry scissors in my catch-all kitchen drawer, their appearance engenders a swift, pleasant reminiscence. She used them to create her perfect crust. The scissors are grimy and I have left them that way. She would never have allowed them to remain in their present condition, but in her eighties, with eyes failing and dementia encroaching, the dirt did not annoy her. Even now, I can see her right thumb and index finger looped into the metal holes of the pastry scissors. The tool is heavy and cumbersome but can still cut a piece of wax paper, and I suppose, pastry as well, although I have not tested for that.

When making the pie, she would carefully place the homemade pastry into the bottom of the metal pie pan and smooth it up the sides. She used the pastry scissors to cut the excess hanging from the pan's edges while her left hand moved the pie tin in a clockwise circle, ever so slowly. Then, she crimped the top of the unbaked crust. The remains of the pastry became parts of a cross-stitched cover for the top of the pie. When she took the pan from the oven, the red cherries—darkened by the heat—bubbled and peeked through the golden-brown lattice. She decreed that pie was best served warm, after exiting the oven precisely 45 minutes earlier. In addition, pie was eaten without ice cream, lest the precious crust become soggy. The sole person who could ignore both edicts without any retribution was my sister's husband Tom, the son-in-law exemplar who could do no wrong as far as Mother and Daddy were concerned.

Looking at my hands now, I see hers. They are about the same size with similar, gnarly fingers. Clear nail polish usually covered her nails; mine have not seen polish for decades. She wore two rings–her modest wedding ring with three, small diamonds on the left and a handsome, purple Alexandrite stone set in gold on the right. This ring was a gift from her friend Eleanor Kelly when I was born. I wear a similar combination, although I am not legally married. My ring includes a diamond from her wedding ring.

☾   ☾   ☾

Mother was an enforcer of rules and a believer in punishment. She sometimes used a hairbrush on my rear end (ouch!) or soap on my tongue (perfumy and slimy!) but more often, she required multiple handwritten lines. In one noteworthy instance, I wrote, "I will not put *moussaka* under the cushion on my chair." I had done that and immediately forgot the deed, hence, it was there for her to discover in its rot. That was 100 lines.

When Mother hauled herself out of Manistee to St. Paul, she tried to leave behind the limitations of her upbringing but it was impossible for her to escape the influence of her semi-evangelical Lutheran background. Evangelical Lutherans followed a set of rules that rejected worldly pursuits, personal adornment, dancing, and alcohol. They practiced absolution of sin through confession. She rejected these tenets but her moral compass of people's behavior could be harsh.[38]

She tried shame to change behaviors. She inferred people were less than commendable if they did not mend their ways. She blamed her much-loved brother Ell's death from diabetes on his love of ice cream, and she criticized my first tooth cavities on my love of chocolate bars. An evening's second scotch and soda could make her husband an alcoholic in her mind.

As a young adult of 27, although I was no longer writing penitent lines, Mother's opinions could enrage me. I wrote:

> *Mother was at her most self-righteous, wanting to reform American society of Wonder Bread and greasy hamburgers. She is the ultimate Puritan. I have long since learned to ignore this side of her. She is a difficult person for me to like, surely not someone I would take into my confidence in many things, yet she has supported my intellectual pursuits completely & while not understanding my emotional self too well, she has put up with it. What can I say, she is my Mother and by virtue of being so, she means many things to me.* (JPS journal, March 18, 1976)

She did gradually soften her perspective and developed an appreciation of psychology and an understanding that some behaviors resulted from disease. She became an advocate for family planning. Before *Roe v. Wade,* the District of Columbia offered medical abortions, and she helped pay the medical fees for two, young women who were part of our extended family.

Mother read Betty Freidan's *The Feminine Mystique,*[39] which provided firm evidence for her belief that women held the short end of the stick. The book presented an upending of many ingrained mores that she had experienced and struggled to accept. Mother planted seeds of Feminism in me and affirmation that a woman could find her own path, choose the traditional format, or embrace a combination of the two.

---

38 *Finns of Michigan's Upper Peninsula.* The Finnish American Heritage Center. Arcadia Publishing, 2018.
39 *The Feminine Mystique* was published in 1963.

Although Mother did not have her own career during my childhood and adolescence, I profited from her ministrations as a mother and her determination to provide me with a college education.

According to Mother, Daddy, and other relatives, I was a sweet child. Belying these reports, I bloomed into a brat at age eight. There were a lot of Mother's rules that I found hard to follow. Mother offered a poem on my 21st birthday that captures her experience of me as a child.

> *Now it might be said*
> *That at times one wondered*
> *Had someone blundered*
> *Or how develop*
> *That mighty strain*
> *As a little one went*
> *Stamp, stamp*
> *I won't go to camp.*
> *Or, I'm taking my suitcase*
> *And leaving.* (1970)

My father was the soft touch, which I figured out early in life. In his long absences due to his work, I could more easily adore him. He could be induced to slip me some extra cash, although Mother tightly controlled the household money, and accompany me to McDonald's to relish the Forbidden Cheeseburger! As for Mother, I thought of her as distant and I dreaded her judgment.

> *As a child I used to feel that my mother was unfair to my father and I always sided with him. Perhaps as a factor of age, my sympathies have become more aligned with her in some kind of psychological balancing act. I can see that the very things which delighted me as a child in my father are the very qualities which bother me about him now. And the various things in my mother which drove me wild as a child are more pleasant/understandable*

to me now. I guess one never really completely loses one's childish relationship to one's parents. Probably one just starts to understand the bonds and frustrations a little more. It appears as if Daddy is becoming more difficult in his old age and that Mother has mellowed considerably. But this observation is fed no doubt by the same balancing act. (JPS journal, November 24, 1974)

My parents were older than my friends' parents by a significant margin. If Mother had a sense of being older, it rarely prevented her from trying to keep up with her younger daughter. In India, in my 11th year, she rode sidesaddle on a carousel with me. The carousel was a rickety excuse for an amusement park ride. Once we chose our mounts and the ride began, the operator kept increasing the speed. He might have misinterpreted our shouted pleas to slow down as encouragement, or he might have been evil.

The adventure turned dangerous when Mother slid off her wooden horse and shot into the air. I saw her land with force against a nearby wire fence. Then, alarmingly, she disappeared from my view. Still spinning, I caught only brief glimpses of her on each full circulation of the carousel. I started to cry. I thought she had hurt herself and that it was my fault. When the carousel came to a stop, to my surprise, she was waiting for me. She gave me a hug and let me know she was okay.

Despite our philosophical and emotional agreement about a woman's place in society, I never could tell her I was dating, much less whom. Similarly, I did not tell her that I was taking the birth control pill.

☾   ☾   ☾

In 1947, my parents and sister (age seven) moved to Athens, Greece, as part of the Marshall Plan, a component of the Truman Doctrine. My father's knowledge and expertise regarding the US labor movement were solid credentials for his job, which was one of the most fascinating he ever had. Greece was in sorry condition following the war. The Nazis had wrecked its institutions and infrastructure, and it was not safe initially to travel outside of Athens. Mother had the charge of finding permanent housing for the family, which was not as easy as it might sound. In 1982, she wrote,

"After Business Comes Friendship," a synopsis of her experience. She submitted the piece to several magazines without success.

> *The men went to the Mission*
> *The Kids to school*
> *while mammas researching housing*
> *learned*
> *how upper-class Greeks*
> *lived.*

She explains further:

> *Mostly, I looked in Kifissia, a lovely summer area with many trees and gardens, the mountains in view. One day I joined one of my fellow shipmates. Outside of an old Finnish woman in my childhood days who in search of a free night's lodging sat by our kitchen stove in Manistee, Michigan contentedly puffing her corncob pipe, my house-hunting friend was the only other female I had seen smoke a pipe. As we came upon a spacious one-floor bungalow set in a large garden, Mrs. Tutt, with me tagging behind, walked up the long garden path to the door, rang the bell, and said to the servant who answered, 'We're Americans, and since we need a house, I'd like to have this one.' Naturally, her request was immediately granted.... Many of the Kifissia landlords were eager to rent, but just for the summertime. Also, we were looking for a furnished house with a furnace fueled by oil if possible and a 'deposit' on the roof for water. The German General Rommel had emptied most of the supply at Lake Marathon Dam and sent it over to Africa to supply his troops.... Also, we became quite accustomed when we inquired, 'Do you have a <u>cul de feu</u>—a furnace?' to have the prospective landlord/lady throw open a shutter and exclaim, 'See the lovely view, isn't the sun warm and beautiful—poli aurea?'...*

And here she writes of my entry into the family.

Of all our four Greek houses plus several hotel stays in-be-
tween, our happiest days were at the Andresaki 'spit' [house] be-
cause there Jill Penelope joined the household. You guessed it, she
arrived following a torrential rain, through which Alan and
Heatherbunch drove me to the clinic, on a Sunday midnight, Sept.
14, 1949. She was a big, happy baby. Alan gave the Greek olives
credit for her birth. There were a number of babies born in Greece
to us Americans. . . .

We used to put Jill on the porch to sleep and try to keep
the dog on alert. Amalia [our housekeeper] always said, 'You
must watch out for the gypsies, who steal babies.' Maybe she
was right because one day I came on one looking down in Jill's
basket. . . .

We returned to Washington, DC, in 1953.

Mother primarily wrote self-styled, free-form poetry. For my 45th
birthday, she gave me these handwritten words:

Happy Birthday, Jill
and many, many more.
Perhaps we've never told you
At that time
Gypsies were a threat, and
Folks said, 'Beware, gypsies
might come and take you away'
and
One day as I looked
from our kitchen window
to the porch where you lay
There stood a Gypsy woman
admiring you, our child,
Well, let me tell you,

We soon chased her away
So that you are here
Today!

The poem was presented on formal stationery. I framed it after she died, and it is now in my bathroom where I read it almost every day.

Mother and Me, c. 1951

Mother tried her hand at opinion and essay pieces; a few were published. She labored over accounts of travels and family life and produced the Strachan-O-Log periodically. The Strachan-O-Log endeavored to capture significant events in our family's life against the background of political and international events. It was like a letter that might accompany a Christmas card but she issued it several times during a year.

One mid-September day
we began a trek
from East to West
North to South
then back to East
by way of kith and kin

who invited us in
to chat and chin,
to eat, and sometimes sleep
while oft the troubles of the world
we tried our best to solve.
(EBS, December 1982)

Neither my sister nor I were a fan of these reports. I thought them unbearably corny and embarrassing.

Inspired by trips to Greece over many years, she penned on a scrap of paper:

In ancient days
Greeks sang lays
Pondered while
behind their backs
they fingered beads.
Yes, they were men
until women came
and to all that said AMEN.
(date unknown)

Written while traveling in Spain in 1975:

Don Juan had his Leperello
Don Quixote his Panzo [sic] Sancho
But 20ᵗʰ century man
Thanks to Women's Liberation
Must think his docile mate
A mere hallucination.

Mother's diaries reveal her to be a keen observer of the physical world and she dutifully chronicled her observations and points of view without flowery language. If she did not achieve a daily entry, she wrote steadily. For car trips, she kept a specific diary where she logged daily mileage, places visited, picnic lunch menus, and whatever she saw from the passenger seat. Daddy did the bulk of the driving.

> *9/26/73—beginning mileage 39,734. From Bonar Bridge, Scotland. 9:15 AM—Beautiful day. Quite large hydroplant. Lonely, yet public tel. . . . A stream struggling along. A rainbow in complete arc with its shadow across the mts. Sun on the right & rain on the road at the left. Low mts all around. Crofters [farmers] appear to have new living arrangements as their cottages of stone are deserted & we see only the sheep. . . . 9/27/73—beginning mileage 39,909, leaving Ullapool.* They drove 175 miles the previous day.

Her diaries contain the facts, "Just the facts, Ma'am," as Sergeant Friday often said in "Dragnet." Here are a few entries drawn from three months during her life in Lahore, Pakistan, which illustrate the range of her interests.

> *July 29, 1961, from Lahore, Pakistan. Last eve. Jill & I went to hear Walter Hautzip, an American pianist, but obviously a refugee from Vienna, play. . . . Very good program—Brahms, Beethoven, Bartok, Chopin. Enjoyed him immensely as he has a very lyrical quality. Poor man had a virus with accompanying fever but kept his engagement. The sweat was running down his nose. . . . Jill & I had a long swim before lunch with the pool practically to ourselves after Mr. B & his basset hound left. Temp 100 degrees.*
>
> *August 13, 1961. Late I finished & late in my life 'Lady Chatterley's Lover.' It really is an encyclopedia for sex. But beautifully written. I don't know how many of us attain this sexual accomplishment and fruition. It is something to aim at even in this busy, frustrating world. No doubt it has a class basis in English society because the lover is a gamekeeper, but I should think that he has the basis for a mature character & both he & Lady Chat-*

terley show character development in their desire to overcome the obstacles in their path for an accepted life together & a home for the child. Lady C. without a happy warm sexual life was a warm personality, going thin & depleted.

September 15, 1961. While in Karachi, read half of the 'Cambridge History of India,' Supp. Volume, The Indus Civilization by Sir Mortimer Wheeler, 1953. [Although she does not say so, I would imagine this was not a beach read.] *Some interesting points in the climate of the Harrappa & Mohenjadaora Civilizations.*[40] *'Human factors can within certain limits produce results which centuries hence might easily be taken for those of true desiccation.' Unlikely basic climatic changes responsible for deterioration in agriculture in Indus Valley. Some change in rainfall in 4,000 years but human neglect or interference (evidenced by baked bricks). Salt incrustation—if the subsoil waters were absorbed, as it once must have been by the roots of trees & crops instead of being constantly lifted to the surface by unimpeded solar action, the crust would not be formed to anything like its present deleterious effect.*

On September 19, 1961. Positively sick to my stomach with the news that Dag Hammarskjold [Swedish economist, second Secretary General of the United Nations] *had been killed in an airplane crash in the Congo. . . . What this will mean to the World Situation, the United Nations as the moderator, one can only speculate.*

As a boarding student in seventh grade, I was separated from my parents (1961–62). Daddy was on temporary duty (TDY) in Karachi and Mother on home fires duty (HFD) in Lahore. I went stateside early so as not to interrupt my school year. They planned to return to the US in December 1961, instead, they came home in spring of 1962. For my senior year (1966–67) while they were living in Sri Lanka, I was once again

---

40 Mohenjo-daro was built in the 26th century BCE. It was one of the largest cities of the ancient Indus Valley Civilization, also known as the Harappan Civilization, which developed around 3,000 BCE from the prehistoric Indus culture. Source: Internet.

a boarder and lived in the same boarding school room that I had as a seventh grader. After high school, I went to college in Chicago. Their tour of duty ended in summer 1969 and they returned to Washington, DC.

During these periods, Mother wrote to me two times per week. Judging by the cache of letters she saved, I was a consistent respondent, even as a young person. In high school and college, our letters contained exchanges about people, my conditions in the dorm, politics, my course material, and money, but never about family relationships, boyfriends, marriage, or anything intimate. The letters sometimes provided her a teaching opportunity, which she embraced with grace and wit.

From a letter dated July 1, 1967:

> *Darling, may we suggest again that when you make an accounting of expenditures—you do it as follows:*

Date	*Balance on Hand*	*$*
"	*Rec'd from my old parents*	*$*
"	*Total*	*$*

> <u>*Expenditures*</u> *(as per your listing)*

Date	*Groceries*	*$31.21*
"	*Party for Alice M.*	*14*
"	*VW repairs (snow tires*	
	Removed as you have	
	Explained)	*16*
	U of Chicago – directories	*2*
	" " "photos	*3*

> *Present Balance on hand*   *$*
>
> *For me, an old-fashioned gal, it is clearer to comprehend.*

She wrote to me when I graduated from high school:

> *We are waiting to hear from you now about graduation and how it went off, how beautiful you looked, who came to the exercises for you, . . . and just all about it because Daddy and I regret very much being so far away. I know you are going to take college*

with a bit of grain of salt—but I hope you will remember that this is not true for everyone, nor can it be because I think higher studies depend on one's facility for them. No doubt you will meet tough competition, but I think the thing is to do the best one can. Daddy and I hope, too, that you will finish the university. I always remember Liz Myers [a friend] . . . who said one day, 'I'm not sure if I got a history masters to wash diapers.' That, too, seems part of a woman's role, to look after children when they are young. But I have found that even when one is ironing, one can think of many things besides what a beautiful job you have done on a shirt. Or perhaps you will be in the class, even in the US, to afford some of these things done, but the way of the West is to know how to do all these things. . . . You girls are part of a new generation that should have cognizance of world affairs—for myself I hate these female conversations that are just centered on children and household affairs. And let me add that often I think with the mess in politics and world affairs, it is about time that woman began to put her hand to the wheel. I know I have done little except to try to keep abreast of what is happening in the world, to try to remain alert—and the rest I guess I just pass on to you and Heather and your generation. All in all I think Daddy and I have lived a pretty full life—we have had our bad times, mostly economic during the depression days and even when Heather went to Pembroke I counted the pennies. We have been a part of the growth of America in world leadership. (EBS letter to JPS, June 9, 1967)

In the summer of 1968, when I was 19, Heather and I descended upon the then-family homestead in Colombo, Sri Lanka, for a stay of one month (for my sister) and two months (for me). Heather traveled with two women friends and I with one. Mother put together a Strachan Harem Tour, as she called it, and we five young women, Mother, and Daddy embarked on a thorough, eye-popping tour of Sri Lanka in two cars, visiting two game parks, tea plantations, old hill towns such as Nuwaraeliya, former British guest houses, the pilgrim town of Kataragama, and Kandy, the former provincial capital and the site of the Temple of the Tooth Relic, one of the most sacred places of worship for Buddhists. Kandy hosted the annual Perahara Festival.

Kataragama is a sacred pilgrimage town for Buddhists, Hindus, and the Vedda, who are indigenous Sri Lankan. In Sri Lanka, I observed on several visits in 1967–68 and 1996, that the distinctions between religious faiths were comfortably fluid with few unswerving, rigid lines among them. If Sri Lankans traveled from their home to another town, they, whatever their faith, would respectfully make the rounds of the Buddhist and Hindu temples as well as the Catholic church.

August 12, 1968 (Evelyn Strachan's journal). The entry covers a journey in Sri Lanka from August 6 to August 12.

We saw no fire-walking at Kataragama but one man swinging with 7 hooks in his back plus innumerable small pins in his arms. There was no blood and the skin is somehow loosened. Others had arrow or pins through their tongues, one was being pulled by a hook in his back, several stood on nails. The crowd was in a frenzy. There were dancers of all kinds—Kandy [Kandy dancers are highly stylized and instantly recognizable by their movements and clothing] and many similar, but what was different was the rather large untrained group with peacock feathers and a kind of yoke over their heads. With Bernard, the chauffeur, we joined hands and made our way down to the temple of Ganesha. We went inside the courtyard where some elephants were waiting and Maggie and Heather were taken for a peek inside by an English-speaking man, . . . the pushing crowds bothered Jill and I stayed with her. We had taken off our shoes as the sign said, but Bernard did not enter. We were the only Westerners there and quite conscious of the people's stares. When I sat on a pedestal of an elephant head, a pilgrim asked me to move saying 'This is not nice to sit on a sacred place.' So, I said 'Please forgive me.' . . . The worst part was getting out against the crowd. That was the only time I was afraid. Jill was very unhappy about the situation the

*next day and it was partly my fault for not warning her of what
to expect, so we did not push our way to the temple the second night.*

Mother's description is accurate to my memory, including my discomfort throughout the evening's activities. I was unhappy that night.
Given a similar opportunity now, I would not take it. I would give a
"rational" reason for declining; I suppose. Clearly, I am not a duplicate
of my mother; to begin with, I lack her insatiable curiosity.

On the same trip, Mother recorded an encounter along the road
with pilgrims who were on their way to Kataragama.

*They had been walking for days. One woman was carrying
a baby and one young woman, about 30 but rather fat and looking like a black mammy had her feet bound with rags. They must
have been sore. All the people, as in Kataragama, raised their hands
above their heads and called out 'Aroa-roha' or something similar
which evidently means 'Praise be to God.'[41] Then a wisp of a man
with a straw hat, toothless, and carrying a bunch of peacock feathers
came lightly bounding out of the forest.[42] He looked like Papageno,
the bird man from 'The Magic Flute.' We had got out of the car
and Bernard said he was a fortune teller, by palms. We learned he
was also a farmer with three acres of land. He, too, was in route to
Kataragama. So, we had our fortunes told. . . . With Heather, he
asked 'Is she a student?' Her studies would be interrupted. When
H said, 'Oh, but I am going to finish,' he took an old ring off his
finger, put it on hers and said a charm. Then he looked at my hand
and cried, 'You just missed being born a queen. You have no enemies
only friends.' When I asked how long I would live, the answer was
20 years.*

---

41 More likely, the pilgrims were saying "Haro-Hara" (from Sanskrit)--a chant to invoke the God
of Kataragama. Perhaps the pilgrims were traveling as part of the "Pada Yathra," which is an annual
"religious walk" from Jaffna to Kataragama. The feet bound in rags suggest a long walking journey.
Source: Sri Lankan friend.

42 Heather recalled that he ate the whole banana without removing the skin. I remember this detail
as well (even though I was not there) because Mother included it in her oral recounting of the
encounter, even though she doesn't mention in her written account.

Heather completed law school without interruption, despite getting married in December 1968. Mother was 61 when "Papageno" told her fortune, and she outlived his 20-year prognostication by nine years. Back in the US, Mother, perhaps as a nod to Pagageno, purchased a lovely, purple chair with wide arms that bore a resemblance to a throne with its back piece shaped like a protective shell. It was no ordinary recliner. After dinner duties, she happily transformed into Queen Evelyn, sitting upright in its embrace to read.

Heather's friend Susan wrote Mother a thank you note.

> *To Mrs. Strachan, We went over a bridge at Kataragama and you said, 'Well, it's not as good as Benares[43], but it's pretty good,' as we glanced at the people wading in the sacred river. You are unmistakably the queen of your household, kitchen and realm whatever it may be—even though the peacock man from out of the woods said 'No'. But in reference to the 1st comment quoted above: May I nominate you also queen of the understatement and thank you for all the planning that went into the Harem Tour.*

Mother was not employed during my lifetime, but I have slowly come to know that her life experience was an instructive force for choices that I have made. I did not seek her advice nor honor her for who she was. It was easier to dismiss her. I flinch when I recall the many times I adopted Daddy's opinion about a topic without considering the value of hers. I am sad that it took me 50 years to begin to appreciate her intellect and the full measure of her love and care for us and her friends. Cultural and social mores played their part but I accept responsibility for my behavior.

There are all types of activists and Feminists and I count Mother among them. We stand on the shoulders of the women who came before, have pushed for more, said no, and told their stories. It is breathtaking to consider the cumulative impact of all these experiences across all the ages. The powerful still treat women dishonorably, and they do so with conviction.

My mother understood me better than I ever acknowledged while she was alive. Similarly, she loved me more than I could understand. She offered my sister a nuanced explanation of me.

---

43 Now called Varanasi. Also known as Benares, or Kashi, it is a holy city on the banks of the river Ganges in Uttar Pradesh, India.

Jan. 23, 1976

My Dear Heather:

Here is Jill's new address and telephone number. It is just as well that you have it as who knows you might need it in an emergency....

The other evening you said that Jill could call you at any time. Of course, she can and will. But she has very little money to use for long distance calls even to her sister. Jill, as you know, values family relationships. This is understandable as for the past six to eight years most of her association has been with students coming and going at all academic levels. Then she is not married, and this may make a difference. This is why I suggested you call her when we were talking the other evening.

Much love,

[Mother]

The moment when I first experienced the full intrepid, loving power of my mother was the night in February 1980 when my parents and I were engaged in our second conversation about my coming out. Daddy was angrily insistent that I leave their home immediately. It was my mother who convinced me to stay. It was she who, after that night, took the initiative to rebuild bridges of communication between us. Daddy and I were both too hurt and too stubborn to take the lead.

She was not done surprising me. Alan, her beloved husband of 63 years, died on November 13, 1996. At first, her dementia kept her from realizing he had died. After the second nursing home roommate to occupy his bed departed, her strong, clear will resurfaced. She made the choice to refuse all food. We did not attempt to change her mind but honored her decision. In her dying, she took charge of her destiny. It took three weeks for her to accomplish this final goal on March 21, 1997.

Evelyn Berglund Strachan

(1907-1997)

☾   ☾   ☾

The last words belong to Walt Whitman.

For his birthday on August 6, 1943, Evelyn B. Strachan gave her husband, D. Alan Strachan, Leaves of Grass, which comprises all the poems written by Walt Whitman following the arrangement of the edition of 1891-92 (Modern Library, New York). She wrote, "To Alan, With love and best wishes on 'Life Begins at 40.'" I choose Whitman's poem, "America," an 1888 addition to Leaves of Grass, Book XXXIV, "Sands at Seventy."

> *Centre of equal daughters, equal sons,*
> *All, all alike endear'd, grown, ungrown, young or old,*
> *Strong, ample, fair, enduring, capable, rich,*
> *Perennial with the Earth, with Freedom, Law and Love,*
> *A grand, sane, towering, seated Mother,*
> *Chair'd in the adamant of Time.*

Evelyn B. Strachan, c. 1950

DIAGNOSIS: LETTER NOSTALGIA

HANDWRITTEN LETTERS and notes provide a window to the soul that email and emojis cannot open. In his memoir, *Growing Up*, Russell Baker describes his mother and her suitor using "the mails to shelter their loneliness" during the Great Depression.[44] Although I grew up in another time, that was me, myself and I. Letters were my shelter for loneliness. They were a joy to receive unless they brought bad news. I responded rapidly but thoughtfully, relishing my connection to the other person.

Letters brought me affirmation that someone cared enough about me to write to me. In contrast to the tenuous quality of email communications, physical letters have solidity and permanence. And a misplaced letter subsequently recovered and reread frequently provides a flowing tap of sensations.

The paper's texture is telling. As a survivor of the Depression, my mother invariably used the thinnest onion skin paper to write more words at less cost, especially for international mail. Until recently, I saved most of her letters. After reading a good portion, I found homes for them with family members who remembered her or something she

---

44 Russell Baker, 1982. His autobiography of growing up in America between the World Wars.

wrote about. Others are in my closet and still more are in a larger archive devoted to the spouses of foreign service officers. Some found a resting place in the trash can because I could not keep them all. I was ladened by several layers of sadness at their disposal. After my demise, there will be no similar collection of epistles nor a dutiful child to take on sorting. I plan to release what remaining letters I possess into the universe but the moment and method are yet to be determined.

Letters written on lined notebook paper might reveal that the writer has at that moment thought of the intended recipient and torn off a sheet to pen a few loving and quick lines expressing their fealty. The letter's unexpected arrival makes the heart skip a beat. Similar letters could deliver news of an old friend, contain a gift of an unanticipated check, or a bill from a former roommate that finally found its way to the proper recipient, which would be me.

Aerograms are letters written in haste and mailed immediately. Generally, they do not require postage because their purchase includes the cost of air mail, although depending on the destination, additional postage could be required. Air travel and World War II boosted the use of these air mail letters. They are also enclosed in their own envelope, which the writer constructs by correctly folding, following instructions printed on the aerogram itself. Once one successfully either seals or opens them, which requires a delicate, experienced touch, they are very efficient, although limited in function. They can be hard to read because the writer often crams words onto the limited space. I wonder, does the use of aerograms connote the sender has only this number of words to write to the recipient? The recipient could expect a long letter and be disappointed to receive this thin and, depending on the handwriting, hard-to-read alternative.

The writer's scent, absorbed in the paper, might waft ever so slightly to the inquiring nose, and thereby rewarding the forlorn lover. Heavier paper of quality reflects purpose: "Thanks for the job interview," and love: "I really mean what I am writing to you."

In early letters, though I am not an artist, I drew a simple face or a flower for emphasis. Or, I added a sidebar in the margins. Unless I copied the letter over, my readers could see any corrections I made to grammar and spelling and draw their own conclusions about the status of my literary preparedness. A willingness to share less than perfect prose and handwriting showed my comfort with a recipient.

Now, the plethora of typos and grammar mistakes in emails are a testament to what? Expediency at the cost of clarity? Some people apologize with a note below their signatures, "Forgive my typing. I am using a tiny keyboard." Even these explanations occur less frequently than they did at the beginning of the magical smart phone craze, as if none of us need to worry about valuing expediency at the cost of everything else. People seem to be saying "Please, people we are very busy people. You have no idea."

I have not mentioned the color of ink and the type of pen. Favoring black ink, I used a fountain pen for a while, its fatness in my fingers brought a comforting sensation. I used blue ink, too, and aqua, red, and pink with ballpoint, felt tip, and markers. My "scientific" survey shows that letters in black or blue ink in my possession survived in envelopes inside drawers, boxes, or foot lockers. There is no home cure for coffee-stained masterpieces; no painstaking reconstruction can restore the blurry images represented by smeared ink. Typewritten letters usually emerge in excellent condition, even when produced on the sheerest of onion skin, and assuming they met no mishap along the way.

A letter and its envelope form a cosmic package. They contain emotions and details of lived lives. We once used air mail envelopes and affixed 26-cent stamps (1974) for international transportation, assured they would arrive in a timely fashion. We avoided chancy surface mail, which took much longer. Correspondents wrote messages on the envelopes such as "SWAK" or "Sealed with a Kiss." A writer might entrust a forgotten thought or instruction to the envelope's back flap. Now, we affix stickers to support our favorite nonprofit or the nonprofit that recently sent us return address labels in thanks for or in hopes to elicit a donation.

Reading old letters whisks me into a world no longer in existence. There is both joy in reading them and sorrow, although not necessarily in equal measure—a treasured friendship remembered sparking renewed contact, a liaison gratefully forgotten, emotional slights relived, personal challenges laid out bare, political events digested anew, a job offer proffered, an acceptance to college, a death revealed.

During one of their separations for my father's career, Mother sent him these thoughts in a letter dated April 28, 1966. She had just turned 59 and he was 63. They had been married for 33 years.

I see you sometimes do read the same things that catch my eye, like the studies on geriatrics, not a particularly nice word for old age. It seems to me that there was so much nonsense written about what happens to a gal (note this term in my youthful feeling of the moment) after menopause that it seemed as if she might as well go and jump in the river. True you can't have children, but then most people have had them by then, but I frequently find myself wishing for you. I am sure the drive does not come as often, but still it's there. While on the other hand, I sometimes think what an old crone I must look, still I feel often I can do things because I think people cannot consider me on the make, that I can talk to people I otherwise might not were I much younger. Age must have some compensations.

Her paragraph is a tribute to their vital connection that spilled out over six decades. Speeches at anniversary celebrations are not as poignant, and I believe email, which they never used, could not have conveyed their intimacy and knowledge of each other.

Responding to a deeply seated emotion, I eagerly await the supposedly daily (except Sunday) mail delivery. Where I live, the mail delivery is spotty and is becoming even more random. In my mind, I draft a letter which is more like a rant to the postal service. "Dear USPS: Guarantee five days of delivery and leave it at that. Promise me no more the swift completion of appointed rounds, since it is no longer possible for mail to arrive despite snow, rain, heat, and gloom of night, as the postal carrier's motto proclaims it will. Sincerely, Jill P. Strachan. P.S. I understand that even if the USPS were to deliver as promised, there is little likelihood that any personal letters would be included. For that I do not hold USPS accountable."

Sometimes a letter, but more likely a postcard, peeps out from bills, fundraising solicitations, and bulk mail. People still send holiday greetings, stretching the season from November to March, but these missives are less likely to contain a note of greeting than a printed account of past year's happenings. I cannot understand the reason and expense of sending holiday cards that do not include a handwritten message. Even, "Sincerely, The Smiths" in handwriting would be a welcome personalization. Otherwise, I am forced to think that a printing establishment executed the mailing project with no affection involved. Imagine a Valentine's Day card without a handwritten signature . . . incredibly sad, that.

I do not know exactly why I stopped writing letters and keeping a journal. There were many factors from efficiency to laziness to technology, but despite my ingrained habit, I stopped writing in my hand. It was a seismic culture shift that few of us resisted.

In second grade, my teacher forced me to hold the paper in a specific position and write in a slant to the right, even though my mind and body did not agree. The same teacher summarily flunked my handwriting. In response, I created my personal script, which developed over several years and which I now use to write checks and to send notes of congratulations and condolence. It has degraded over time but is generally legible. However, my partner Jane asks that I narrate the grocery list as she takes notes in her own indecipherable script.

The right-hand drawer of my handed-down wooden desk of 35 years is a storage place for notes, letters, funeral programs, photographs, and other writings of interest. It is easy to tuck unclassifiable, unsorted keepsakes there and I cull from it occasionally. It is a single drawer and although about 18" inches wide, it is not tall. When the drawer gets too full, papers start falling out the back onto a shelf that runs across the underneath of the desk.

I came out to my parents in October 1979. Five months elapsed from the moment I spoke the specific words, "I am gay," until our second and last conversation on the subject. During that time, we exchanged two letters but we did not use the postal service for delivery. We lived in the same city and handed the letters to each other. We affected gestures of nonchalance but anxiety was rife.

I did not want to reread their letter but my arm refused to throw it in the trash. Because I had no other plan, I tossed the letter and the copy of my subsequent response into my right-hand drawer. Once in the drawer, the letter radiated its location. While I was looking for another piece of memorabilia, I detected it. Even if I touched it or moved it, I never reread it. The letter was a basket of betrayal and utter sadness, and it embodied an unexpected break from my parents that we never wholly healed.

Finally, in 2017, I searched for it in the drawer but it had vanished. I doubted that I had thrown it out or if I had, I hoped that I would have remembered. I supposed that it had ended up in a different place within the apartment, still signaling its existence.

I found the letter when it was least expected but sorely needed. Thirty-six years after it was written, the letter and my parents' sentiments were intact, there to be read with my eyes and touched by my hands. I cried as I had in 1979.

☾   ☾   ☾

Across any distance, a handwritten note projects a flutter of intimacy that's unimaginable in our sterile e-world. A hundred frowny faces can't console the grieving widow like a single piece of stationery on which a friend inscribes her sympathy. The temporal images of Snapchat can't drive the pulse like the arrival of an actual love letter, in the flesh. (Ron Charles, *The Washington Post*, February 12, 2019)

That's the letter. I started it Wednesday when you
were reading in the bed & before Paul got here. I threw
the original away when Paul got here because it was
such a crappy feeling to write something like that, and
I couldn't and did not to concentrate on it and he
was a good excuse to chuck the whole thing. About
that same time I found a poem. I thought you'd appreciate
it, but I didn't show it to you, just because.

ACROSS THE TABLE AT BREAKFAST

You join me half-awake, half sleeping,
Settling down to the chair as if into bed.
The affection of your dreams for you last night,
which has smoothed your face, drains fast
through my clang of dishes, the gurgle of
coffee. Soon, half full of breakfast,
you will utter your first unchosen words.
They will come between us like children,
hands in their pockets, with nothing else
to do. And then they will take sides.
                        GREG KUZMA

It could be worse. It will be better.
                        Pete

Last page of Pete's letter, March 21, 1973

7 HANOVER TERRACE
REGENTS PARK
LONDON N.W.1
AMBASSADOR 9393

27th May 1969

Dear Miss Strachan,

I admire Joyce, Kafka, Beckett, Dostoevsky and
Shakespeare.

All the best.

Yours sincerely,

Harold Pinter

Letter from Harold Pinter, May 27, 1969

"LED GO! YOU ARE HURTIG BE!"

FOR 30 years I called my father, Douglas Alan Strachan, "Daddy." I do not recall the reason but assume the endearment's origin lies in my baby-speak. There came a time when I could only refer to him as "my father." My anger toward him created a painful distance between us and I could no longer respect and love him in the same way. He had been an accepting, understanding father but he ultimately rejected me. My anger shaded my feelings and it took a long time for me to break through to a new nuanced understanding of the person who was my father.

☾   ☾   ☾

I had a pleasant childhood graced by my parents' solid, friendly relationship, their shared adventurous outlook on life, an older sister to look out for me, and many singular experiences stemming from living abroad from birth through my teenage years. Daddy loomed large in my psyche from the start. His sense of humor was at the ready and I enjoyed his company. On Saturdays, when we lived in the US, he would spend several hours in his workroom and, as a young child, I liked to watch him while he rewired lamps, fixed small appliances, and built furniture.

Around the age of seven, I heard someone use the common phrase, "You can say that again." I tried it out on Daddy, and he repeated without hesitation the exact words that he had uttered a few seconds before. He followed with a big smile. This tickled me, and I looked for other opportunities to get him to do the same thing.

He read Rudyard Kipling's *Just So Stories* at bedtime. I particularly remember his reading of "The Elephant's Child."[45]

> *In the High and Far-Off Times the Elephant, O Best Beloved, had no trunk. He had only a blackish, bulgy nose, as big as a boot, that he could wriggle about from side to side; but he couldn't pick up things with it. . . . The Elephant's Child had 'satiable* [meant as insatiable] *curiosity, which led to his unfortunate conversation with a crocodile by the river. As the crocodile pulled on his nose . . . the Elephant's Child was much annoyed, and he said, speaking through his nose, like this, 'Led go! You are hurtig be!' . . . When his nose became nearly five feet long, he said, 'This is too butch for be!'*

Daddy read the voice of the Elephant Child through his nose, as if he had a severe cold, and perhaps as Kipling intended. His spot-on interpretation always kindled laughter from me, and I enjoyed his reading it again and again.

Heather's favorite book, the title of which is long forgotten, had a central character named Jon, which Daddy pronounced "Yon." The "authorities," Heather and Mother, told him that Jon was pronounced the same as John but he ignored them. I remember several discussions at dinner on this point. Begrudgingly, he agreed to pronounce Jon as John, but in his inimitable style, he still got the humorous upper hand. Every time he had to read Jon's name out loud, he would say, "Yon pronounced John." For a children's book it was lengthy, and Daddy had set himself an unrelenting

---

45 Our illustrated copy from 1951 called the story "The Elephant's Child."

task. As a fan of Laurel and Hardy, Charlie Chaplin, and Harold Lloyd, who Daddy championed as grand artists, he was up to the challenge.

In family discussions of political and current events, we were occasionally divided. Mother and Heather constituted one cohort, Daddy and I the other. I adopted his point of view without hesitation. Given my age, it is unlikely that I understood the gist of the matters being considered but I took pity on him for holding his point of view by himself.

One friendly argument surfaced from time to time about the name of the city in Yugoslavia (the country dissolved in 2006) where Mother, Heather, and Daddy had seen a well-dressed man walking an enormous pig on the sidewalk. He guided the pig by hitting its side with a long stick. The three of them were driving from Greece through Yugoslavia to England in 1951. I was not present but was sure that Daddy was correct in remembering the city as Belgrade (now in Croatia), whereas Mother and Heather insisted it happened in Zagreb (now in Serbia). I defended him on this point for no reason other than my emotional attachment to him.

Daddy and Me, September 1983

Daddy enjoyed the company of women and they enjoyed him. He was not a Feminist but he lauded the achievements of his Aunt Ella; Eleanor Roosevelt; Esther Peterson, an advocate for workers, women, and consumer rights; and Frances Perkins, the longest serving US secretary of labor (1933–45). He acknowledged their successes but he was untroubled by women's limited professional mobility. He felt comfortable with women serving in secretarial positions, although he undoubtedly helped a few women move closer to the glass ceiling during his career.

Some of these women, many of whom were single and who worked with or for him, became family friends. Their attachment to him became Mother's, who kept a lively correspondence with them and made sure they were not forgotten. Margaret Mary Davies (1912–2007) became a professor at Seattle University. The subject of her PhD thesis was the work of the American Mission for Aid to Greece post WW II, in which my father played an important role.

As for his daughters, my father was supportive of our academic and professional success. Without a son, his fatherly energies[46] were directed to us in sports, woodworking, and mechanical endeavors, and my sister became accomplished in the last two. When she married US Representative Tom Foley in 1968, Daddy's attention diverted to Tom. His constant focus on Tom and his career prospects was irritating to me.

He and Mother shared a traditional approach to the duties of marriage, influenced no doubt by the societal underpinnings of their era. He was the breadwinner and Mother was the homemaker.Yet, she always managed their money and expressed her opinions, which did not always match his. When she maintained her point-of-view, he would remind her she had believed the "talkies" (referring to movies with sound) would never succeed. Many of their discussions ended with this demeaning putdown.

Yet, Mother could share her ambivalence about her role as a housewife with him.

---

46 With thanks for Maria Popova's thoughts on Florence Nightingale's father "with the countercultural impulse to give his daughter the same education as he would have given a son." *Figuring,* pp. 212--13. Pantheon Books, 2019.

In retrospect, I wish I had made the effort to get a degree.
Of course, look what you have done without it, but you might say
yours was a lot of in-service training. . . . I have been reading The
Feminine Mystique, a recent much-discussed book by Betty Frie-
dan, in which she states, ... since the suffragettes made so many
gains, women have deteriorated by moving out to suburbia, hav-
ing too many babies, etc. . . .

Summarizing Friedan's suggestions that women find mental space
to pursue nonhousehold duties, Mother continued.

The trouble I find is that too many gals really don't want to,
and one tends to be looked askance if one is interested in what is
wrong with the world. (EBS letter to DAS, October 18, 1965)

Daddy loved her and us. When he was separated from us, he wrote
faithfully, concluding his letters with similar sentiments to these:

What I would do to hear old Jillybunch recite 'The Night
Before Xmas' or to get into a first-rate argument with Heather
about anything is more than I can tell you. What I would do
to see you and the kids at this moment is—well—well—words
cannot explain. . . . With lots of love to all of you and please give
Heather and Jill an extra big hug for me. And take a super one
for yourself. Love, Alan (DAS letter to EBS, March 21, 1954,
from Korea)

Just before Heather and Tom's wedding in December 1968, Daddy
shared with Esther Murray, Tom's aunt, his sentiment about the incoming member of the family.

Perhaps I should welcome it most of all having been surround-
ed by females for so many years. (DAS letter to EM, November
30, 1968)

After he retired, with pressure from Mother, he reluctantly assumed a few household duties that he turned into an opportunity for accolades, which he cheerfully accepted if anyone were inclined to provide them. When I visited them in Washington, DC, while I was in graduate school in Syracuse, he offered a commanding demonstration of how he made the bed each morning. It was delivered in jest but with an undertone that suggested housekeeping was unimportant. I could not stop baiting him on this issue.

> *I must say I was a little taken back where you say in your last letter at the very end, "Daddy, are you helping Mother...? ... You know I'm Mother's little helper all the time. You seem to have some reservation on this subject, apparently. What am I doing when Mother is washing the breakfast dishes—a very simple task requiring no particular skill or imagination? Making the two beds, a job which, on the other hand, requires great skill, patience, and, as I have discovered, physical output. Even Mother admits I make a first-class bed. . . . So while Mother is preparing dinner (a more or less routine operation), I am cutting the fresh beans French style. Mother even remarked that for someone with a cauliflower ear,* I cut a mean bean. I trust this gives you a thorough understanding of how I am helping Mother. Of course, I could go on—who is it that is the only one who can clean the carpets, take out the garbage etc.* (Letter from DAS, March 13, 1974) *Cauliflower ear was Mother's pun calling out Daddy's selective hearing.

Daddy's charm was irresistible, and it prevailed with me up to a point. It became frustrating when I realized it functioned as a coverup for what lay within him. But his charm was still going strong in my twenties when I wrote to my friend, Peter Biella.

> *My hair is much longer (well, probably not) and I have it in a ponytail today. My father likes it that way, because it reminds him of when I was 10 and wore my hair in a ponytail, and to see*

me this way, makes him think he is younger. . . . I don't like my
hair in a ponytail, but I'll wear it that way because it makes my
father feel young, and I want him to feel that, because he is. (JPS
letter to PCB, December 1970)

☾   ☾   ☾

Daddy struck a dapper pose remembered for "his white hair, pipe, and soft English accent" (sympathy card from Cousin David Berglund). Born in London, England, in 1903, he entered a modest household preceded by his sister Molly, who was born in 1902. After the birth of his brother Stuart in 1907, their parents divorced. John Meffen Strachan, their father, committed suicide in 1918 at 44. He was an alcoholic. I never heard Daddy speak of his father, my grandfather. As a teenager, I found out about his suicide when Mother told me, and she stressed secrecy.

After his parents divorced, the young Alan and his siblings and their mother, Minnie Alma Conboy, moved into one house with several aunts to pool resources. Auntie Ella was a buyer for a London department store. Her salary was essential to the financial well-being of the household, although others contributed. Daddy adored his Auntie Ella.

In their new home, the children had a terrier named Mr. Pip, who was the smartest, cutest dog that ever lived, according to Daddy. Upon command, Mr. Pip could toss a cookie up in the air from the bridge of his nose and catch it in his mouth. He also laid in wait on a chair for the cat to pass by, at which point he would bat the cat's tail from above. There were few occasions in Daddy's life when he was dogless. He did not mind when Mother, Heather, and I teased him that his eternal lot was to be in the company of women. But to reassure him, we reminded him that our dogs were male and that he should never feel defenseless with Trigger, Ouzo, Nicky, or Dizzie by his side.

Attendance at the new neighborhood's Church of England was a Sunday family event. Family lore recounts that when the priest visited Daddy's mother to inquire why Alan was no longer serving as an altar boy, Daddy proclaimed, "There is not a touch of Jesus about the place!" Perhaps he unwittingly illuminated the significant difference between high and low Anglican churches, assuming one is ever in need of a handy explanation. Despite his boyhood concern, Daddy did not become a loyal adherent of Anglicanism, regardless of high or low.

Daddy's mother went by Alma, her middle name, a practice inherited by her two sons. Alma was the name of a major battle in the Crimean War (1853–56). A family wag, maybe an uncle on her father's side, teased that she was lucky her parents had not named her after Sebastapol (now known as Sevastapol), a better-known skirmish in 1854.

After the divorce, Alma began dating a chorus member in the D'Oly Carte Opera Company. He courted her with tickets to Gilbert & Sullivan (G&S) productions at the Savoy Theater, and she brought her children along. This was an enormous luxury and resulted in Daddy's exposure, along with that of Molly and Stuart, to music, theater, and singing. Alma sang *Pinafore's* "My gallant crew, good morning" to her children at the beginning of the day, and their sung, "Sir, good morning!" resulted in breakfast being served. My grandmother did not marry the cast member but instead, she followed her three children to the US, where she died in 1953.

G&S brought joy to family gatherings well into the 1970s, when we would stand around the piano with Molly playing and singing alto after divvying up the other parts among family members. Daddy had a musical baritone and Uncle Stuart was an equally melodic tenor.

Although Alma (I called her Grannie) died before I knew her, one of her favorite expressions circulated in our household. When asked what was for dinner, she always replied, "Knobs of chairs and pump handles." Mother applied this response to Daddy's daily query about the evening repast. It was the perfect repartee for someone who rarely took part in creating a meal.

Daddy emigrated to the US in 1926 and became an American citizen in 1934. A touch of his homeland was always present in his knowledge of English literature; love of G&S operettas; passion for cricket, tennis, and soccer; and a honed, deadpan humor. Because he had learned literature by rote, he would pluck a relevant poem, passage, or saying from his brain to adorn a story or situation. After toying with becoming a professional cricket player, he left England because he did not feel that there were economic opportunities there. At 5'11", he was an excellent athlete but he lost many of his teeth playing soccer. Daddy suffered from asthma year-round, and he had a rough time of it in late August, when ragweed blooms. But as a master of the disguised drop shot, he played tennis until the age of 83.

He knew how to swim but did not find it fun. His fair skin was not at home in our postings to hot-weather spots. Sometimes, though, he would join us in the water. His bare chest revealed an enormous scar that ran the length from his collarbone to his waist. I inquired of my mother; I had learned early in life not to ask Daddy an embarrassing question, and she told me that when he was a child and ill with a cold, a doctor applied a hot mustard plaster to his chest and left it on for too long. When they removed the plaster, it took his chest skin with it. Mustard plasters were a regular remedy for congestion, aches and pains, and arthritis in the early twentieth century.

Four months after Daddy arrived in the US, Auntie Ella died unexpectedly over the Christmas holiday. His Aunt Classie wrote to him:

> *Dear Auntie sank rapidly in the afternoon & passed away peacefully with her hands in Molly's and Stuart's. Your name was the last word she spoke, so she must have been thinking about you, Alan. She looked so happy after her death & so young & if anyone deserved eternal happiness it was Auntie. She spent her life in trying to [illegible] others & was one of the noblest & best woman in the world. Everyone loved her & no wonder. . . . Now my dear boy I know you will grieve but you must try not to grieve too much. . . . Although we cannot see—everything is supposed to be done by <u>the will</u> of God for some good purpose. There's one thing we do know. 'Our loss is her gain.' She is free from all ___ Sorrow. You would have felt that if you could have seen her after she died.*

She really looked lovely–so calm & peaceful with such a sweet smile. She looked quite happy. (Letter to DAS from Aunt Classie, January 6, 1927)

D. Alan Strachan in England, c. 1925

Having arrived in Detroit, Michigan, with a six-year apprenticeship under his belt, Daddy had the papers to prove that he was a qualified "fitter and turner," but in this different place, he discovered they called these workers "tool and die makers." Tool and die makers are skilled artisans who produce precision metal parts, instruments, and tools. They work in machine shops, tool rooms, and on factory floors.

Daddy was a self-made man.

The product of a divided family, I was an unhappy and rebellious adolescent who without the approval of my parents quit school at fourteen, at that time the legal minimum age in the U.K. . . . A six-year apprenticeship to one of the country's lead-

ing electrical manufacturers, which my parents despairingly ar-
ranged, resulted in my becoming the first member of my family to
acquire a trade. But leaving school at fourteen left a crucial gap
in my formal schooling.[47]

A reference letter from The British Thomson-Houston Company,
Limited–Electrical Engineers and Manufacturers:

> *26ᵗʰ July 1926*
> *Mr. Allen [sic] Strachan.*
> *This is to certify that the above mentioned was engaged by this*
> *Company from 16/9/18 until 6/10/25 when he left entirely of his*
> *own accord, to gain experience as an Apprentice. He served a full*
> *term of six years satisfactorily and was given a charge hand's posi-*
> *tion during the last year of his service with this Company. He was*
> *at all times a painstaking and studious workman and his general*
> *comportment was all that could be desired. [signature illegible]*
> (A charge hand is a worker in charge of other workers, but the
> position is below that of a foreperson.)

My father's first jobs on the factory floor shaped his worker's perspective, which was fundamental to him as an organizer of the United
Auto Workers (UAW). In October 1943, he came to Washington, DC,
to serve on the War Production Board (WPB) as director of the automo-
tive division and a promotion to WPB deputy chair followed.

His diplomatic career began in 1947, when he became the labor ad-
visor to the American Mission for Aid to Greece, part of the Marshall
Plan, which sought to address Europe's economic challenges after World
War II. This was perhaps his favorite career posting.

In a 1989 interview with the US Department of Labor, he expressed
his zeal for the administrative challenges, his colleagues, the Greek people, and the visible outcomes he brought to fruition during his six years
serving in Greece. He influenced the organization of the Greek labor

---

47 D. Alan Strachan. *From Picket Line to Protocol-Recollections of a United Auto Worker.* Binder #2,
p. 376. Unpublished. 1985.

unions, which the Germans had devastated during World War II. The American Mission helped establish vocational education and apprenticeship programs while consulting on the policy level.[48] He had retired 16 years before in 1973, and his Greek experiences had taken place 40 years earlier, but they were stamped on his memory.

In October 1953, during the McCarthy era, Harold Stassen, who was a perennial Republican candidate for the presidency and director of the US Foreign Operations Administration and special assistant to President Eisenhower, dismissed Daddy from his job without explanation by means of an international cable. Stassen summoned him back to the US within 30 days. Stassen was a staunch anti-Communist and perhaps took umbrage at Daddy's connections to the labor movement and the Socialist Party. It took 22 months to achieve reinstatement as a government employee and he lost accrued benefits.

His subsequent diplomatic posts in Pakistan, Egypt, and Sri Lanka provided stimulating background for our family life. He also served in Vietnam from March to November 1965, administering the US foreign aid program. Dependents could not live on post because of the war.

I came to disagree with my father about the Vietnam War. It was a difficult topic to discuss, although our heated conversations did not divide us from each other. My college years (1967–71) occurred during periods of protests against the Vietnam War and the draft. A prolonged strike on my campus interrupted academic life. Daddy and I kept on talking about foreign policy and the war; he with extensive knowledge and me with anti-war passion that college life had engendered.

His last assignments brought Mother and him back to Washington, DC. Upon his retirement in 1973, after many years of secretarial support from his staff and Mother, Daddy reacquainted himself with a typewriter because he wanted to write a memoir of his life in the labor movement. It remains unpublished and is now stored in two binders on my bookshelf, with additional versions in boxes in the garage. He and Mother lived a lovely, retired life just shy of 20 years before dementia took over.

---

48 US Department of Labor, Bureau of International Labor Affairs, "Rebuilding Labor and Democracy in Postwar Greece: An Eyewitness Account," April 1989.

My cousin Elliot, who grew up in Minonk, Illinois, a small town of 2,000 folks, recalled him:

> . . . *there were a few special visitors that brought the rest of the world to our house. . . . But no one visiting had the grace and charm of your Dad, with his wonderful accent and colorful past. I always knew the tennis would be full of finesse and the dinner conversations enrapturing. Alan . . . inspired me in my formative years and will always be with me.* (Letter to JPS from Elliot Gregg, January 21, 1997)

Daddy was an avid raconteur, and he turned his many experiences and encounters into amusing tales. In 1918, on the first day of his job at the British Thompson Houston Company, known as BTH, he went to the men's restroom.

> *Arriving at my destination, I timidly opened the door and entered. In front of me, written on the wall in box-car letters was this evangelistic and revealing statement:*

> *THE WAGES OF SIN ARE DEATH BUT*
> *THE WAGES OF*
> *THE BTH ARE A BLOODY SIGHT*
> *WORSE THAN DEATH*

> *Thus at the tender age of fifteen, I was introduced to the class struggle. Ten years later, when working in the tool room of the Ford River Rouge [Michigan] plant, I happened to mention to a fellow toolmaker my concern about the economic gap that separated the workers from the wealthy was growing wider. He thought about it for a moment but dismissed further discussion with 'What the hell. When I leave this dirty factory, wash-up, change my clothes and go out for the evening, you can't tell me*

from Henry Ford.' The class struggle meant nothing to him.[49]

   But leaving school at fourteen left a crucial gap in my formal schooling. The Socialist Party helped fill the void. It unfolded to me the world of political idealism, explained many of the mysteries of economic theory and practice, the need to educate the electorate, the struggle to obtain social justice, and the importance of international understanding. Meanwhile, my wife [Evelyn, my mother] had become a professional social worker. Before long she had convinced me that such people as Freud and Jung were not kinky shrinks, as portrayed by radio and vaudeville comedians, but progressive social scientists who were spearheading new theories for treating mental disorders.[50]

   Although I am no longer a practicing socialist, I can never forget the influence the Socialist Party played in shaping my thinking and approach to life. Apart from introducing me to some of the most interesting and genuine people I have ever met, the Party not only educated me but implanted in my mind a discerning conscience that I use as a reliable yardstick for measuring the social conduct of individuals, organizations, political parties, and governments. Whereas others rely on religion as a guide and spiritual comforter, I have chosen democratic socialist idealism as my secular conscience. . . . Although I consider Socialism to be an impractical political theory, it is however a philosophical mind opening force for inquiring into the principles of human behavior and social problems.[51]

Daddy was not shy about telling his stories and was happiest when they involved persons of some notoriety. His unpublished book is rife with anecdotes about UAW leaders Roy, Victor, and Walter Reuther, Leonard Woodcock, and Emil Mazey.

---

49 Strachan, Ibid. Binder 1, pp 14-15.
50 Ibid., Binder 2, p. 377.
51 Ibid., Binder 2, pp. 384-85.

I need not remind you that Alan, Walter, and I were com-
rades in the early struggle to build the UAW. Alan never forgot
his roots with workers, and during the war against Hitler and
the post-war rebuilding Alan remained loyal to his heritage. The
knowledge of the dedication of his life to the service of others should
help relieve the pain of his loss. To you and all in your family,
All of us in the surviving Reuther Family send their love! Affec-
tionately, Victor G. Reuther (VGR letter to EBS, November 20,
1996. Victor Reuther died in 2004.)

⟨   ⟨   ⟨

All this is just so much prelude to recording The Event—
my coming out to my parents. The details are still clear in my
mind—e.g., suggestions of psychiatrists, my arrested develop-
ment, my lack of fulfillment, indeed, my lack of womanhood.
I doubt I will forget the experience anytime soon. But was I ever
ready! I was/am proud to be me and unwilling to flinch because
of it. I am proud of myself and have only gained strength from
the experience. But things are not the same. But I also believe
that those weird vibrations will disappear with time. (JPS journal, October 23, 1979)

Beginning in my twenties, my relationship with my parents became
more like an exchange among adults. We had fun traveling together, and
we shared interests in music (including Mozart, Harry Belafonte, and
The Beatles), theater, politics, tennis, and dogs. Yet, we never discussed
my romantic involvements, and I identified no one as a boyfriend or girlfriend. They never asked. It made no sense but I was more comfortable
thinking they would figure it out.

Over 10 years, I brought home several boyfriends and my girlfriend
Lynne, who moved to DC with me in 1977. My parents loaned us the de-
posit and first month's rent for our one-bedroom, basement apartment.

When Lynne and I parted ways, I reported her departure but could not reveal my despair because I was not out.

Leaving a Large Clue such as H. Montgomery Hyde's book, *The Other Love,* by my bedside did not draw forth parental questions. The cover of Jill Johnston's boldly named and graphically presented *Lesbian Nation* did not raise any eyebrows, either. Nor did mysterious, long phone calls with Lynne.

My parents always welcomed my friends. It was a point of pride for me that my college friends admired them. Two of my friends lived with them when they started new jobs in Washington, DC. Others sustained their own connections through letters and phone calls. Part of my parents' appeal was their politics; they were less conservative than the parental norm of the 1960s. My friends enjoyed the dinner table conversations about Democratic politics, humor, and Daddy's stories.

Out of self-respect and respect for my parents, I decided I had to tell them I was a Lesbian. The feeling grew from a "what if proposition" discussed with friends to a gale force within me, and I could not ignore it. This happened in October 1979. I wanted to be wholly honest, so I made my first statement in person at their home in Washington, DC. I had spent many school breaks in its lovely, comfortable confines that included art from their life abroad and mid-century modern furniture, in which my sister had schooled them. This was the home where I had taken part in lively dinner parties with good food and excellent conversation.

It was a tough evening. We had no common tools with which to engage in a discussion of this importance. We plunged into these waters, and, despite a history of relatively good communication, we became mired in emotions. I wanted my parents to accept my self-description but their first response was to offer to pay for a consultation with a psychiatrist. As a trained social worker, my mother held great store in psychiatry. She believed in its powers to fix people, including alcoholics, wife deserters, unhappy housewives, and homosexuals. Daddy's own ideas on these topics had expanded through her tutelage, thus, he tagged along with her ideas and theories about people's behavior.

I agreed to go if they would join me but they declined. Thereafter, every topic of conversation during dinner contained an uncanny but seemingly unplanned reference to psychiatry or a psychiatrist. We were stuck in a revolving door, unable to extract ourselves. Trying to lead conversation away from the obvious, I inquired about the affairs of family friends. When I asked what a ballyhooed son was doing, I discovered he was in medical school studying psychiatry. *Why not?* In turn, they asked similar questions. My old college roommate, what had been her major? Psychology. *Of course.* It would have been hilarious if it had not been so agonizing. The hindsight of many years standing is much funnier. We did what we did best as a family by navigating diplomatically through dinner. Driving the short distance to my apartment, I was in shock at my parents' reaction. I had prepared myself for defending and explaining my choice but not for rejection.

An exchange of two letters followed. We did not use the postal service but delivered our missives by hand. Perhaps Daddy thought his letter too personal to trust to regular means, and since his letter was the first volley, I followed suit. In Daddy's letter, dated December 10, 1979, he claims full authorship. I did not receive the letter until late January. To my query about its delay, I was told they postponed delivery to "preserve the holidays."

His letter began:

> *For better or worse I find the best way for me to face your bombshell of October 10 (1979) is to put my thoughts down on paper. In so doing I hope that you, who have brought so much joy and pleasure into my life, will at least respect the concern I have for your future. So here goes.*

Alarm, sprinkled with love, dominates Daddy's typed, five-page, single-spaced letter. Since there were no typos nor grammatical errors, I figured Mother must have served as editor, typist, and proofreader.

My announcement was a game changer in my relationship with my parents. It was my own "bombshell" to discover my parents misunderstood me, and that in their eyes I would become an embarrassment if I did not change my behavior. Daddy believed homosexuality was abnormal. With my declaration, I forced him to apply this term to his younger daughter.

> *The experts maintain that somewhere in the background of physically normal individuals who choose homosexuality as a way of life, there will be evidence of retarded development—a failure to come to terms with the natural relations between the male and female species. . . .*
>
> *My purpose in writing like this is not to shame you into changing your position. Neither is it directed to your emotions. . . .*
>
> *Your Mother and I are not strangers to being members of a cult. During the years we were in the Socialist Party, we lost most of our former friends. We seldom went to the theatre or listened to good music and only read literature of a socially conscious nature. For about three or four years we lived in this small community ignorant of what the rest of the world was thinking. The cause we served was a worthy one—the building of a more equitable society. To us the cult with which you have chosen to identify yourself is one for advancing the selfish sex preferences of two similar individuals at the agonizing cost to themselves, their parents, relatives, friends, and the future of civilization. It is difficult for Mother and I to see how you are benefitting yourself by 'copping-out' on your worldly responsibilities. . . .*
>
> *During your college years you have introduced us to many friends of both sexes—some of whom we have entertained in our house. Can we be blamed for speculating whether they follow your lifestyle? . . . Mother and I find ourselves in an ambiguous position with respect to these friends of yours. . . .*
>
> *One very important matter you failed to make known to us. Do you intend to become an active participant in the 'gay' liberation movement, or do you prefer to keep it private? It is necessary that you tell us. . . . What about Heather and Tom? The family? Friends? Stop and consider. What do we say should any of them ask embarrassing questions?*

*Jill, please, please, understand that we love you very much
and always will. You are still our younger daughter who used to
make delightful cooing sounds in her cradle;....*

My announcement called almost everything into question. I worried I could never enjoy my parents', particularly my father's, company again. Based on our first conversation, I feared banishment from their warmth and unflappable security. Their reactions signaled irreconcilable differences that would separate us permanently. But I was not willing to change my spoken words.

My response, dated January 30, 1980, was a letter in black ink using a ballpoint pen in long hand, on three-hole, punched, notebook paper. Copied over from an edited, handwritten draft, it was just under two pages. Unlike entries in my journal, I took pains to make my handwriting as clear as possible because I did not want illegibility to contribute to further misunderstanding.

> *Dear Daddy and Mother,*
> *I have read Daddy's letter several times and find that there is much in it to which I might respond. But this letter is a response to the premise on which Daddy based his argument.*
> *My gayness is not and has never been a political statement. It is the way I am. It is I/me.*
> *The only choice I faced in relation to being gay was to choose to accept myself as I am or to choose to ignore myself as I am. And the latter choice, of denying my self-understanding, was never a possibility.*
> *So the facts are simple. I am gay. There are no quotation marks around that word for me.*
> *Because my gayness is what I am, there is no possibility of it being a political choice akin to socialist, Democrat, Republican, feminist persuasions. Your attempt to understand me in that light denies the essence of what I truly am and ignores the emotional aspect of me. That is too bad, because my emotional self wants you*

to understand and accept me as I have come to understand and accept myself.

When I say I am proud of myself, I say so with the knowledge which comes of self-awareness. I have looked in the mirror and been not ashamed of what I saw. I know my self-awareness has opened up worlds of human possibility. I know my friendships are more meaningful than ever before and that I am loved and respected because I have had the courage to face myself. By this I do not mean I know myself completely—that is why we live—but I mean that my acceptance of what I am has allowed me to reach emotional meanings essential to my life experience. It is because I came to accept myself that I wanted to tell you about me.

Situations such as you describe happen every day and could happen to me. [In his letter, he expressed concern about my ability to have a career, a family, and friends if people knew I was gay.] *I know I am not immune. But there is no other option for me. I could deny myself and opt for success and be assured only of unhappiness. Even then, there is no guarantee that such a course would bring me career success. And there is so much more to life than that! At some level, your arguments about my job and future are irrelevant. They do not apply to the central question of life—whether to accept or deny yourself as you are. Since I believe that this coming to terms with oneself is so important to the living of a whole life in which there is sharing and understanding with loved ones, the reasons for denying my self-understanding which you list are secondary. Please know and accept that it is* not *that I am caught up in an adventure of the moment, it is* not *my political ideology. It is that I am gay.*

As I mentioned in October, I am not the result of one incident, one philosophy, one cause. There is no way to explain the way people are, ultimately, they are. We spend our lives searching for the parts which constitute the sum of our separate existences. And I am what I am. I could not ask for better parents. As individuals, I admire much that I find there. Because I care for, love, and respect the two of you, I ask you to accept me.

*I would be happy to talk further with you. It is very important
to me that we continue to try to communicate for the many reasons
I put forward in this letter.*
    My love,
    Jilly

Our second and final family conversation about my Lesbianism occurred in February 1980, and it was tumultuous. Once again, I sat in my
parents' living room feeling unsteady. Margo, my dog, was my companion. Daddy started, "You saying you are what you are is just a bunch of
bullshit." Well, maybe he did not use that exact word, but it was something close. I protested. He slammed his left fist on the arm of the sofa
and yelled at me to get out of the house. I got up, retrieved my coat,
and put it on. My excess energy propelled me back and forth from the
hallway to the living room while I fumbled with my coat buttons. I was
crying and yelling, and Daddy was doing the same. We upset Margo with
our noise and obvious discord. She loved the three of us, and she ran
around trying to calm us.

Mother was in tears, and she pulled at my sleeve from her seat in a
woven, straw, side chair. She implored me to stay, saying, "Daddy doesn't
mean what he's saying, he's just upset. Please, please, please." Now
dressed for the outside, I acquiesced by sitting on the opposite side of the
living room from her. We were in a triangle with Daddy at its highest tip.
Conversation continued following the arc and themes of the first; they
repeated the entreaty that I go see a psychiatrist. Again, I offered to go
with them but stated that I was not changing who I am. They declined
to join me.

I stayed for dinner because Mother asked me.

Eventually, Margo and I returned to our basement apartment. My
bed that night was a Medieval rack and I tossed and turned. Several times,
I panicked, thinking that Daddy had a heart attack and that no one had
called me. Once or twice, I sat upright in bed to check on Margo to make
sure she had not stopped breathing. At 5:30 am, I went to work. My first
phone call that evening was from Mother. She was checking on me.

Mother became the mediator, and my father and I became objects of her mediation. I cannot say for sure, but I believe this was a role change for both. Maybe she was always mediating behind the scenes, as women have often done, and maybe he was not the gentle giant that he appeared to be when I was a child listening to him read "The Elephant's Child." Maybe he was not the fun father who would eat cheeseburgers with me and give me extra money without Mother's permission. Maybe he was not the father who talked about ideas and politics with my friends and me. Nor was he the affirming person who championed my educational efforts and career to his friends.

My Journal, April 1, 1980:

My parents . . . for the first time today I wondered if I should have told them. Then, I wondered if the fact that I hadn't felt that before was a defense reaction. I have continued to feel sad about this today. I have caused them a lot of pain, most of which was inevitable. Yet I had to do what I did—I know that. The hardest part for me has been to come to terms with my perceptions of them, in fact, it's really only my altered perception of my father. It's great to find my mother supportive, if new and different in terms of my perception of her, but much harder to deal with the fact that the patient paragon of virtue known as my father is in fact an angry and unresolved man. Was I blind not to see?

Even with Mother's intervention, we could neither hear nor listen to each other.

Forty-one years on, I am still connected to the sentiments I expressed in my letter, with one caveat. Our family was neither emotional nor demonstrative in our caring for each other. In my letter, I could have done a better job of describing my parents' irreplaceable importance to me.

I know my letter had too many "I am what I ams" or versions thereof. I had recently seen the film, *"La Cage Aux Folles,"* and it resonated with my thinking and writing. The movie was a window into the life of a gay person, complete with shame, drama, conspiracy, compassion, and enduring love. It is an unblushing story of two gay men entertaining their straight and accepting son, his fiancé, and her conservative parents in their very gay-a-fied apartment above a nightclub featuring drag acts. As a French-language movie, it was not expected to be well-received in the US but its cultural and political impact was astonishing in the late 1970s. It was both a hopeful and revelatory moment that a story of this kind could have a happy ending. I sang its signature song, "I Am What I Am" in choral concerts and it became a national Pride anthem.

It is easy for me to see now how someone who was spouting "I am what I am" could not understand someone who was appealing to common sense. Pitting emotion against the practical is not a recipe for successful communication, or, from "Cool Hand Luke," "what we have here is a failure to communicate." This is fun to cite but not much fun to live through. It is odd that Daddy took such exception to me insisting "I am who I am," however, since he was certainly who he was.

(((

It is painful to acknowledge that our separate lives spun out another 17 years without serious or profound discussion about much of anything. Once, in my office, talking on the phone with Daddy and looking down onto 14th Street, NW, he asked me if I planned to take part in the March on Washington; it was October 1987. His interest was a trial question to find out if I was still a Lesbian. When I replied I was attending, he said, "Why would you do that?" I began to explain about the importance of LGBTQ rights but he cut me off. I took solace in the sound of the traffic from below as I controlled my tears. It was easier to stay away from topics that might cause conflict. I had a role in doing that, as did my father, but we became estranged. It was easier to dismiss him than to reconcile with him.

Now, it is clearer to me that Daddy responded from his experience as a successful, self-made man who navigated many odds. His appreciation of what it cost him to succeed made him protective of what he had gained. He viewed my embrace of LGBTQ rights as dangerous and unnecessary. My guess is that he felt dishonored by my life.

Lost time. Gone forever. Heather tells me he regretted sending the letter and he said that frequently--but, never to me. Once dementia set in, the opportunity to do so vanished. I think that is why I have often cried when thinking about the letter. It was so final, even if that had not been his intention in its writing.

Despite or because of the dementia, he expressed anger at me, once shouting from his hospital bed that I had to leave the room and becoming more agitated when I did not immediately depart. That moment was chilling because he was violent, waving his arms around uncontrollably. I called my sister from the pay phone in the hospital hallway and told her I could not visit him again in the hospital.

Why did I wait 38 years, 22 years after his death at 94, to read the letter again? I know I tried once or twice, but I never could get through it because of my anger and sorrow. He had become the distant My Father and was no longer Daddy.

My friend Dan Smith, 21 years my senior, was a source of wisdom on my estrangement from my father. Dan was gay as well, and in his generation, his life was even more distant from his parents than mine from my parents.

> *I remember in both cases of losing, first, my father then my mother, that I felt for a while such relief that I was ashamed of myself. It was only later that I got a better perspective on not only my life with them but their life with me that I fell into a much more charitable and loving set of memories, appreciating them in a more all-around way. I suspect something not unlike that may happen with you. But it takes time, and you have to allow yourself some room for it all to happen.* (Letter to JPS from DHS, Good Friday 1997)

Dan's prediction came to pass. Four years after receiving my father's letter, I could send this greeting, even though I was still angry that his progressive views did not amount to a hill of beans.

> *Dear Daddy—Happy Birthday! This will reach you belatedly. So you have to know that I was thinking of you. 80, hmmm. You've done a marvelous job with these 80 years, touching many people. It must be a pleasure to look back and realize what you've*

seen, what you've changed, and what you've created. I'm glad you
are my father and that I've had the pleasure of 33 of these 80.
Here's to much, much more! All my love, Jilly (August 1983)

 ☾   ☾   ☾

On Daddy's return trip from Vietnam in November 1965, the Department of State assigned him two dozen speaking gigs to "explain" Vietnam and US involvement. He stopped in India, Lebanon, and Greece. He spoke to Embassy personnel, government agencies, and community groups. About his task, Mother wrote, *It will be quite an experience, I should think, to be talking about Vietnam; it's a big job.*(EBS letter to DAS, November 15, 1965). Mother compiled "Excerpts from Letters of D.A. Strachan at Vietnam," a four-page document for close friends and family. I came across the compilation in 2017 as I began going through my parents' many documents.

Reading the "Excerpts" and my parents' correspondence from 1965 brought me unexpected healing. In those letters (each numbered for tracking), I could enjoy the father I knew before I came out. His letters were charming, informative about Vietnam and the politics of the US Mission, sweet and funny. It made me happy to rediscover and to retrieve a fuller picture of him. He had not always been the angry man sitting on the couch yelling at me to "Get out!"

Daddy's letters were factual, but he also wrote about his emotions. He was very lonely when he first got to Vietnam, living in a rented apartment and making do. He planned grocery shopping and cooked his meals, which he did not enjoy. For the first time, he was dealing with household staff, a task that had always been Mother's domain. He had to communicate in his fractured French with a maid who spoke French and did not speak English.

For the first time since coming out to my parents, I had sympathy for him in his telling. It felt better to relinquish the disdain—my protection from profound loss —which had become my emotional, knee-jerk habit about all things relating to my father.

In the summer of 1965, Mother and I were gallivanting around Europe by car, up to the Scandinavian countries and Finland and then down to Genoa, Italy, with stops in Germany and Holland. We ended our trip in Washington, DC. Daddy did not know where we were from one day to the next and letters did not always arrive in consecutive order. Many questions went unanswered, but he kept writing. Mother did the same, hoping that at each stop where the US had an embassy, she would find his letters waiting for her.

These exchanges were unrelentingly positive. They both held this view of life. When separated, some things were challenging, like juggling finances and making family decisions about schooling and next posts. They trusted this shared understanding to carry them through, along with their individual senses of humor. Maybe having survived the Depression was a keystone to their success. Once they got to the other side, they were together as a married couple and intact, as measured by their finances and mutual commitment.

☾   ☾   ☾

Mother and Daddy on a tennis court, c. 1935

Alan Strachan and Evelyn Berglund met while waiting for a tennis court in Windsor, Canada, in 1928. That day, they combined with others to play mixed doubles. They began dating. Daddy felt lucky to have a job, but he was only working two or three days per week. His precarious financial situation in England had brought him to the US, but it took almost a decade for his fortunes to change significantly. An opportunity to join the newly developing Russian automobile industry arose in the early 1930s.

> *For the past three years my girlfriend and I had been waiting for the economic situation to improve so we could get married. The future, alas, still remained gloomy. It was then that I decided to approach my wife-to-be [Evelyn Strachan] with an 'iffy' proposition. If those recruited for work in Russia were allowed to take their wives with them, would she marry me and then accompany me to Russia? Her answer was an unhesitating 'Yes'.[52]*

Mother's response helped Daddy pursue the lead, but although his credentials were acceptable, he was told that the quota was full. This postponed the expected marriage for two years to September 1933. They finally traveled to Russia as tourists in the 1970s.

My parents marked birthdays and anniversaries with gifts and cards, the latter containing bad, humorous poetry:

> *From Alan to Evelyn, April 1987:*
> *Now that your [sic] eighty lets [sic] do it all over again. What do you say? Love, Alan. Look on the Back.*
>
> *Alas, there are a limited number of articles an elderly husband can purchase for an elderly loving wife. It was easier when you were young and needed essentials. In those days I was not embarressed [sic] to give you presents that also had domestic value.*
>
> *But even today I remain hopeless in purchasing women's clothing. Can't judge style, colors etc. In the underwear depart-*

---

52 Strachan Ibid., p. 47.

ment I'm more alert. But this has one [illegible word] handicap. I don't wish to be known as a 'Dirty Old Man' when seen in a lingerie shop.

So please forgive me for the present I am giving you for a most important birthday. Although it does not have domestic usefulness, it can be of great pleasure to both of us.

The Dictionary is on the way
It should be here almost any day
Put to use should not prove scarey
For you to spell Antidisestablishmentary
A pleasant bonus is in sight
We have two reservations for tonight
Mr. Coe speaks well of food and play
Just what is needed for your Birthday

Douglas Alan Strachan
(1903–1996)

In the process of growing older, there comes a time when most of us realize that no matter how interesting and exciting a life we may have lived, it has little meaning in the history of our times. But once reconciled to this inescapable logic, we discover we now have a better perspective for judging the few whose contribution did influence the times.[53]

☾   ☾   ☾

EXCERPTS FROM LETTERS OF
D.A. STRACHAN AT VIETNAM 1985

February 28—*Well, what does it look like to arrive in a country which is in such a state of confusion if not actual warfare? You would never know it except for the large number of GI's around*

---

53 Strachan, Ibid. (1985), Binder #2, p. 381.

*and a certain amount of barbed wire. As we drove from the airport
we ran into a large crowd just leaving a motor bike race. There are lots
of cars around and not old ones either.* . . . *The city [Saigon] itself is
most attractive, with lots of trees and many very nice houses.*

March 7—*A Vietnamese woman who cleans my apartment
(efficiency) and does my washing purchases me some (things) on the
local market. She is diminutive, as are all the women here. Tiny,
small frame, well proportioned, they carry themselves beautifully.
They wear pyjama type trousers and tunic like top with a high dog
collar. The tunic spreads out at the waist into a long flowing garment,
three-quarter length, but is split at the side from the waist. When they
are riding bicycles, these two loose sections blow in the wind. Must say
they are attractive, as are the women who wear them.*

*This is a fantastic city. There are more things for sale on the
sidewalks where on Sundays and each evening the hawkers lay
out their wares than in Cairo. I could buy all the batteries I need
for the transistor radio I had to purchase when we were in Beirut
(many of which we later learned were n.g.)*

March 10—*This morning at 6:45 a.m. I drove to the airport
and boarded a chopper as helicopters are called here. The destination was only about 20 miles away. The chopper has no doors as they
have been removed to allow for a gunner to sit on each side in case
of a V.C. attack. Actually, I'm told there is little chance there will be
one as the only time they really get into action is when they are on a
military mission flushing out the V.C.'s [Vietcong].* . . . *With my
seat belt safely fastened I looked on the countryside 2000 ft. below.
A little frightening at first, but after a while one takes it in stride.*

*The meeting was really something. It was held in the headquar-
ters of the Province Chief—in this case a Lt. Col. In the VN [Viet-
nam] Army. As we came in, the building, formerly the residence of
the French Provincial Director, we were greeted by an orchestra complete with two electric guitars and drums. I thought we had perhaps
interrupted a rehearsal, but no it was for our benefit and continued
playing until the P.C. called the meeting to order at 8:15 a.m. The*

*orchestra played during the short coffee break, during the lunch period
and when we concluded the session at 4:00 p.m. In fact just prior to our
departure it played Auld Lang Syne. Can you beat it?*

*I was much impressed by the P.C. and the representatives from
Saigon who argued the case for the Govt. . . . We came back by mini-
bus over the new super highway which AID [Agency for International Development, my father's employer] built some years ago.
Lots of traffic and plenty of new factories being built in the area as
you approach Saigon. Altogether an amazing place. The Malay-
sian Davis Cup team is here for the weekend. Business as usual.*

March 13—*You should see the traffic here. It's much worse
than Cairo, not because there is more traffic, but because the streets
are narrower and the number of two-wheel vehicles is fantastic.
It's a smaller city for one thing so there are not the distances to
travel. It seems to me that the overwhelming number of people
have their own transportation system apart from the public buses. Bicycles by the dozens, some driven by foot, the bicycle with the
motor attached, the motorbike, large and small, and of course the
scooter. Then there are the push pedal pedicars, the motor driven
pedicars and the hundreds of little taxis. Such a sight you never saw
coming down the road. I will try and get a picture—Makes driving
difficult but as they use the French system that the person to the right
has the right-of-way, nobody stops at corners. Actually, I've seen fewer
accidents here than in Cairo though' the driving is not any better. . . .*

*The situation remains about the same here. No new coups at the
time of writing and the Government issued a very good statement
on its program for encouraging democracy and development. It was
needed but I have no idea what it means to the public. Maybe they
have heard such things before. But obviously the V.C. have all the slo-
gans. They have made the issues and many of them are justified ap-
parently. Actually, the standard of living is high by Asian standards
and certainly India, Pakistan, and Egypt. This mess can be traced to
the way the Commies capitalized on the underground and French colonialism. Who wasn't against the French? So many not communists*

by any stretch of imagination found themselves members of a commie directed and controlled movement dedicated to expelling the French. Politically unsophisticated, can you blame them? After the war, the French attempted to return, but because they had done such a lousy job of training Vietnamese and placing them in responsible positions, it was hard to win the non-communists over the fight against communism.... Perhaps we should never have become involved here in 1955 at the time of the Geneva Conference but it seemed the human thing to do. We gave economic assistance, but we had little to work with administratively, all the people were inexperienced. The commies then began a determined infiltration program country wide, capitalizing on the shortcomings of the various ineffective and corrupt regimes, particularly the Diem one. There is little we can do but defend the anti-communist majority from the communist controlled minority.

March 16—The meeting (in provinces) was very useful to me—gave me a chance to meet the Reps and hear their reports— none of which were at all comforting. The V.C. are infiltrating the countryside deeper and deeper so that the Vietnamese are being driven into the cities and particularly those alongside the coast. It reminds me of Greece. Remember when the only place one could visit were the cities and then only by air or boat? Well, that's the way it looks here. The V.C. really don't want the cities at this stage as cities must be administered and what's even more important, they need food. Moreover, the V.C.'s have to eat so they can't afford to drive everyone off the land. Anyway, we are all pretty well convinced that the biggest problem facing the country will be that of refugees. However, despite this very gloomy outlook, if I could hazard a guess, morale seems to be on the up and should continue to improve provided there are not more coups or rumored ones. The arrival of the Marines has helped as have the air strikes and the capture of two or three boats off the coast laden with guns, ammunition, and believe it or not large supplies of drugs—all made behind the Iron Curtain. If the VN's can destroy the V.C.'s supply lines, the tide will turn. The more frequent use of this kind of equipment, instead of relying upon capturing what we bring here, could be defeating as ours will not fit theirs. There are those, however, who feel this change indicates how strong the V.C. is and now doesn't have to rely on the hazardous and difficult task of raiding for its arms. Time will tell.

Flew to . . . where the large U.S. airbase is located and where the Marines are now stationed. The airport is probably busier than Chicago.

Monday afternoon we flew to Hue. A nice looking city and once the seat of the Emperor. The Dhiems came from there, in fact all politicians of VN come from the central area of the country as does the present P.M. We flew nearly all the way at 10,000 ft. safely above the V.C. Looking down from above, you would never suspect that the lovely countryside was honeycombed with V.C. But it is. Tomorrow early I take off for Region II. This evening at dinner a fellow asked me if he should set me up for a trip to Region IV next Monday. I said no, for by that time I'll have had enough flying and could do with a few days on land. Took some pictures, only hope they come out.

April 5 to Roger D. Lapham *(After serving as mayor of San Francisco, 1944-48, RDL served as chief of the post-war Economic Cooperation Administration for Greece.) The situation is not unlike that of Greece in 1947 when I first went there, though, alas, there is no Tito in the offing in Vietnam. It is the same old story of unenlightened colonialism (French), a period of occupation during World War II by a foreign power (Japan), the formation of an underground which was more interested in building a hard-shell Communist base than overthrowing the foreign occupation forces—defeat of the foreign occupation forces and the taking over by the now well-trained partisans. In the Vietnam case, the French attempted to return so that the Communist controlled partisans had no difficulty rallying the country against the colonialists. A bloody war followed in which many exceedingly brave Frenchmen lost their lives. It ended with the signing of the 1954 Geneva treaty,* *which divided the country into two parts. Since the departure of the French, South Vietnam has not had a chance to establish itself for the Communist trained minority has been slowly but surely eating away at the very vitals of the country assisted, I might add, by the incompetent and corrupt governments which have been in power. Meanwhile, the U.S. has been giving economic aid in an effort to win the support of the people for its government by building a viable economy.*

The Vietnam War officially ended on April 30, 1975.

Daddy, c. early 1970s

ENTER WITH AN OPEN MIND[54]

EVERY VOICE Matters was the mission statement of the non-auditioned Lesbian & Gay Chorus of Washington, DC (LGCW) during the latter half of its 26-year existence from 1984 to 2010. I was a singer and the general manager for most of that period. Our principal administrative tool was a consensus-based process we developed and honed.

In the choral world, making administrative decisions by consensus is unusual, but it was groundbreaking that the LGCW applied the same process to its selection of music and programs. The traditional role of a music director prevailed in rehearsal and performance, but LGCW members actively chose the type of music they wanted to sing. Consensus is organic and best learned by doing; it is not perfect. There are successes, failures, and learning experiences.

Examples of consensus decisions included changing the name of the chorus from Gay and Lesbian Chorus to Lesbian and Gay Chorus, hiring four music directors over two decades, joining a 2002 nationwide

54 This chapter has been adapted from my essay "Consensus in Practice-Reflections" published in The Grassroots Leadership and The Arts for Social Change Corner, December 2020.

boycott of Cincinnati to support Black concerns about racial discrimination and violence in the city, commissioning works, and attending four international gay and Lesbian choral festivals. Commissions and festivals required a substantial fundraising effort from individual members to cover expenses. For festivals, the chorus helped support individual singers who could not cover the full expense to attend.

In 1999, while planning programming to commemorate our 15th anniversary, LGCW members discussed shifting our programming perspective beyond the stories of gay, lesbian, bisexual, transgendered, and questioning people to sing for other people whose voices were unheard and that society ignored. The choice to perform Robert Convery's "Songs of Children" reflected that intention. Convery's cantata was a musical and emotional challenge but singing it improved the ensemble's musicianship.

The context of the piece is astoundingly well-suited to the concept of "unheard voices." Composed in memory of all children who perished in the Holocaust, "Songs of Children" for choir, violin, viola, cello, and piano is a cantata of nine poems written by children interned at Terezin concentration camp.

❨   ❨   ❨

In 1984, at the inception of the LGCW, taking the stage as a Lesbian or gay man was a courageous act. We depended on each other for support in our action. In our first five years, we strongly resisted becoming a formal organization, deciding to delay adoption of bylaws—the first step to incorporation and filing for nonprofit tax-exempt status. We handled business at a half-hour prerehearsal meeting once a month. We understood ourselves in understated terms and because of that grounding, we attracted a music director who envisioned the group in a nontraditional way.

Although not legally organized, we possessed a compelling spirit of commitment and purpose, which are qualities that Mark Bowman admired the first time he heard us sing at an informal celebration. He had studied piano and organ but was forced to give up his dream of becoming a Methodist minister when he disclosed he was gay. Before becoming involved with the LGCW, Bowman had been the choir director at a Methodist church in southwest Washington, DC, and was active in Affirmation: United Methodists for Gay and Lesbian Concerns (now Lesbian, Gay, Bisexual, Transgender, and Queer Concerns). Affirmation is an activist, all-volunteer organization that challenges the bias of the United Methodist Church.

As a favor to a friend in the chorus, Mark originally agreed to conduct one rehearsal; he stayed for six years. He brought a strong sense of personal pride, a seemingly unlimited capacity for grassroots organizing, a deep commitment to social justice, and a vision of what the group could become. He was interested in the opportunity for gay men and Lesbians to work together. Mark's political thinking encompassed Feminist principles and alternative concepts of organizing power. These values helped us build more inclusively on inherent diversity and make thoughtful decisions about our music and organization.

Mark's concept of the role of the music director was uncommon. Although he possessed powerful leadership qualities and the competence to create the organization himself, he used a collegial approach with us. He encouraged us to stake our dreams for the organization on a chosen mission rather than around the personality of the music director.

Mark's perspective was an eye-opener for me. In my family, I grew up thinking my father was in charge with some help from my mother. My early schooling reinforced the tenet of someone being in charge. In my academic endeavors, I operated in a system of clearly identified lords and serfs, which nurtured arrogance. In various jobs, there was always someone to instruct me in the next steps. Of course, I gained a healthy doubt for some authority figures but I never thought my voice was inherently valuable or powerful. I thought I had agency because I had succeeded. Mark's encouragement that we could be different altered me profoundly. I know that through working with him and with the LGCW I discovered a missing piece about being in the world. After Mark moved to Chicago in 1992, he continued to be a good friend and he accompanied me to Pete's gravesite in 2019.

In an interview I conducted with Mark in August 2000, he discussed his relationship with the LGCW and his first observations of how the group operated.

> *My recollection is that when I came to the Chorus [it] was already making decisions as a whole. . . . I don't have a clear recollection of exactly when we decided we were going to continue the consensus decision-making. It was always there.*

Shortly after Mark's arrival, LGCW members articulated the following purpose, which became our mission statement:

> *The purpose of the LGCW is to:*
> *Make quality music*
> *Foster gender cooperation*
> *Demonstrate Lesbian and Gay pride*
> *Develop talent, and*
> *Have fun.*

To create the statement, we used a consensus process rooted in the Quaker tradition, as explained by two of our Quaker singers. An outside facilitator managed the process and agreed to reflect the views and concerns of all present. We pledged to listen and work together to craft a statement acceptable to all. As our growth required, we reaffirmed the elements of our mission statement through subsequent visioning and long-range planning processes, eventually distilling our words to "Every Voice Matters–A World That Listens."

Chorus members were immediately, passionately, and actively invested in the group. We made a formal commitment to a consensus process for our governance. This choice reflected our desire for an egalitarian and just approach to all issues that we might face—allowing for each voice to be expressed and eliminating volatile situations of winners and losers. This decision was Feminist in intention; we believed that our alternative structure would more likely engender sharing of power within the chorus. The choice reflected high, active trust within the organization based on a common purpose: to sing. There was a group consciousness of what lay behind that purpose: to change the world.

An essential concept in practicing consensus is each person's understanding that *unanimity is not the same as unity*. The group can decide to act (*i.e.*, unity) knowing that there is not 100% concurrence (*i.e.*, unanimity). Each person helps to implement the action to which the group agreed because the action reflects the decision of the group.

In our interview, Mark reflected on the chorus's decision to use consensus.

> *Consensus is not only helpful because it's a more equitable and fair way of making decisions, but it gives people greater investment within the Chorus and I think that's really important. In so many choruses you sort of show up and do what you're told. You don't always understand why things are done or the difficult decisions that go into deciding to do something. The gift of the Chorus was it built people's investment to the Chorus.*

Within the LGCW's understanding of consensus, the role of facilitator was special but not more powerful than anyone else's. Facilitators first alternated between male and female members. Eventually, as the business of the chorus became more complicated, cofacilitators served together for one or two years. They organized internal affairs and represented us to the external world, as well as functioning as listening posts for LGCW members. Around 1990, the LGCW created a second paid, contractual position, that of general manager. The music director was the first. The functions of the cofacilitators remained essentially the same, but the chorus empowered the general manager to conduct operations, a responsibility once shared by the cofacilitators and other volunteers.

It eventually became expedient for many decisions to be made in a monthly meeting for business, rather than a short meeting before rehearsal. We encouraged everyone to attend, but in reality, only a small group of singers did, and this group became smaller as we marked the two-decade mark. The chorus-at-large considered important decisions such as hiring staff and attendance at festivals.

> *NOTE: Remember that Co-Facilitators cannot represent your point of view for you! If you want to express your opinion and give suggestions that can become a part of our decision-making process, we highly encourage you to attend the Meeting for Business.* [LGCW 2005–2006 Handbook]

In June 2000, LGCW members accepted revised bylaws based on the practice of consensus. We had adopted bylaws in the early 1990s because they allowed us to register as an organization at both the local and federal level. Being recognized legally allowed us to raise tax-deductible donations. The 2000 revisions aligned the consensual practice of the organization with its legal documents, which provided an official grounding for the LGCW's value that every voice should be equally empowered within its structure.

☾   ☾   ☾

The story of the LGCW remains for me invigorating and thought-provoking. I was there from the beginning to the end, and I ask myself why it dissolved. I fought hard for its existence and growth for the better part of 26 years. I was LGCW's primary spokesperson, which turned me into a professional Lesbian. It became my way of life gifting me with music, friends, emotional sustenance, identity, activism, professional development, and a monthly paycheck. I cared deeply for the organization and for the people who passed through its "doors." Yet, all my energy was not enough to guarantee its existence.

Since the LGCW's formation in 1984, LGBTQ people have made many strides in creating full, proud lives. It is no longer as remarkable to be standing on a stage singing about our lives. The urgency to protest diminished as LGBTQ people became more comfortable in their surroundings and as AIDS cases diminished in the mid-1990s. Both singers and our audience became less interested in and had a reduced appetite for LGCW's social justice programming.

In Washington, DC, then, an LGBTQ person had innumerable choices for spending leisure time. Competition for people's attention increased and time itself was precious. The growth in the region's population translated into longer commuting times. In our first 15 years, a singer might have been willing to drive a one-hour round trip to rehearsal, but less so when that one-hour trip became two hours. The LGCW started to struggle with recruiting and maintaining singers. As the organization focused on recruitment, its own members began to have diminished pride and faith in its success. To apply a proverb, *Success has many fathers, failure is an orphan.* [Coined by Count Caleazzo Ciano (1903–44)]

Our serious embrace of consensus was, in the end, counterproductive. Our distinctive process tied us down, and we lost consensus's vital organic character. Once named and claimed, there were rules, guidelines, and structures that we dutifully generated and periodically reviewed. A handbook became necessary. We related history and educated ourselves and others, such as donors and concertgoers, on the use of consensus. But the few who were interested became fewer, including a significant number of our singers. They wanted to sing without thinking about process.

Combining uncontrollable factors like travel time with a preference for expediency provides an answer to the chorus's demise. Perhaps it was easier to give up on our consensus process than to find our way back. I am sure I did not understand the depth of our problem at the time. To me, it seemed only that we were battling ennui and competing for people's diminishing free time.

Some of us, like me, had too much ownership, whereas others had too little or none. Once the practice of consensus was associated with only a few individuals, its principles grew more abstract. Despite our many well-intentioned efforts to witness and educate, the power of consensus faded.

In one memorable conclusion to a discussion with an outside facilitator, we stood on one side of the room if we could help with administrative tasks, and on the other side if this were not possible. When the dust cleared, the same people stood on the same sides of the room where they had stood metaphorically and realistically for many years. The helpers were staunch supporters of consensus.

In that moment, the run of the LGCW ended, although it did not disband for a few more years. That happened after reaching consensus to shut down at a meeting for business in 2010. The usual helpers attended.

☾ ☾ ☾

Consensus requires a willingness to listen deeply. When a person commits to the idea that every voice is important, that is, matters, then one must listen. Taking part in consensus-based decisions makes it easier to listen. It is joyful and exhilarating when a group of people acknowledge ownership for a decision. In that case, it is impossible to tell who suggested what, which ideas belonged to whom, and the maxim that the whole is bigger than the sum of its parts is manifested. We all are responsible, and our whole is stronger in its unity. Consensus will fail if individual practitioners are unable to support decisions created by the wisdom of the whole. I promise that it is infinitely more exhilarating and beneficial to work this way and well worth the hard work.

I know that consensus honors the individual voice and the collective voice it engenders. For myself, I make the choice to work in consensus, regardless of surrounding circumstances. Leaning into consensus made me a better manager and worked against my engrained training to decide matters forcefully and without sufficient consultation with colleagues.

The LGCW's work with consensus had a substantial influence on me. My academic and previous work experience had taught me to prove my opinions against the opinions of others. I thought this was a path to career success. Learning about and tentatively practicing consensus created a gradual, gentle change in how I moved through the world.

I notice that the benefits of consensus extend to my personal, work, and group relationships. Being willing to accept the opinions of others without trying to overcome or smash them to the ground in empty victory engenders an openness I had never known or ever envisioned. I found a safe space to be at ease with myself. I discovered an empowering community in the LGCW that made me an intentional listener. I embraced differences and learned from them.

I get along better with people. I am thrilled when I work with others and when we make change happen together.

☾   ☾   ☾

From LGCW Handbook (2005–2006)
Guidelines for Participation in Meetings for Business:
- *Enter with an open mind*
- *Listen for understanding*
- *Make personal statement (I, me) when talking*
- *Take risks: say or do something that may make others, or you feel uncomfortable*
- *Pay attention to assumptions*
- *Take responsibility for yourself*
- *Consider the result of what you are saying*
- *Be conscious of time*
- *Care for yourself*
- *Celebrate*

Consensus is. . . . Well, I can think of what consensus is not. Consensus is not unanimity. Consensus is not all being of the same mind. Consensus is not about the loudest voices outspeaking the quieter voices and winning. In order for consensus to work, it really takes a commitment by the whole group to be part of a process. (2000 JPS interview with Mark Bowman)

**Members of the Lesbian & Gay Chorus of Washington, DC after 1989
GALA Choruses Festival in Chicago**

ROAD STOP NO. 1

1995

GETTING ON the road proved to be the first obstacle for our trip. We set a departure time for Wednesday at noon. Fred called at 11 am to change to 2 pm. At 2 pm, he telephoned again and suggested Thursday. I resisted and, to my surprise, prevailed in getting us out of town.

Fred's Honda Accord, Golda, was in impeccable condition, but that was not the case for her owner. Fred needed more than an oil change and tire rotation to start the trip. Although determined to make the long-planned change of scenery and move 3,000 miles to the west, Fred pushed back on the time of our departure. He was not quite ready to get on his way.

By 4:30 pm, we were on our way to San Francisco, Fred's presumptive new hometown. Never mind that it was the crushing evening rush hour, we headed west with the other cars as they headed to their homes, driving past the Washington Monument, Lincoln Memorial, and Kennedy Center, some of the distinctive landmarks of Fred's hometown for almost two decades. Fred sobbed in the passenger seat.

Fred's positive HIV diagnosis five years earlier had compounded his dissatisfaction with his personal life and job. He was seeking a solution and absolution, and he believed a better life awaited him in the emerald city of San Francisco. He was a close buddy, and I was sad for him to move away, but it thrilled me to accept his invitation to be his driver. I felt special and important, and I loved a road trip. We came to call our time together "Driving Ms. Freddy."

Golda's back seat was packed to the brim with the remnants of Fred's vegetarian kitchen—instant soups, macadamia nuts, stone-ground crackers, yogurts, and cranberry juices, mostly obtained from gourmet supermarkets. A paper shopping bag with handles was the repository of Fred's toiletries—as my mother would have delicately said, even as she would have silently questioned the practicality of the paper shopping bag for its suitcase. These types of items were best squirreled away from public display.

Fred was often late. He was usually meticulous and organized but tardiness did not convince him to speed up. This time, he had been hasty and used a quick packing solution, which was notable. Nevertheless, he traveled with supreme confidence in his ability to find his toothpaste when we stopped each night.

Other crucial items on the backseat were a complete set of tapes of our singing group, the Lesbian & Gay Chorus of Washington (LGCW), recordings of Gilbert & Sullivan operettas, AAA maps and information books, and a national guide to vegetarian restaurants complemented by a similar guide of gay B&Bs. Fred mapped, consulted guidebooks, and read out loud. He controlled the music selections, whether it be cassette tape or radio, although he consulted me in his decision making. After all, we both were committed to a consensus process! We traveled without hotel or restaurant reservations or a phone because it was 1995. We planned to stay in cheap hotels in towns we picked out as we moved along. Fred had given me a car key, which made me Golda's driving superintendent.

Fred and I met in the mid 1980s, during the early days of the LGCW when there were 20 members. Since I was comfortable relating to gay men, it was easy for me to strike up a conversation with him, and soon we were socializing after rehearsal and meeting for periodic dinners.

We enjoyed each other's company, and because we sang in a chorus, we shared many friends and experiences. The same ironies and injustices touched our hearts, and these were frequent topics of our conversations but we also laughed together. We forged a bond.

Fred's HIV-positive diagnosis dismayed me. I had already lost my special friend Pete to this awful disease, and I did not want to repeat the experience.

An hour and a half into our trip, we arrived at our first road stop, the euphemistically named Culpeper Health Care Center in Virginia. The Health Care Center is a place where old people go or are sent, and from which it is doubtful they will return.

**Mother and Daddy celebrate their 50ᵗʰ Wedding Anniversary,
September 1983**

My parents had been residents at this full-service nursing home for 18 months. I avoid the more accurate term, patients. I felt easy asking Fred for the difficult favor of visiting my parents and he had genially agreed since by trading stories about our families, we had constructed a helpful, loving connection. I would have done the same for him had the question come from his side of the court.

My father Alan was 91 and my mother Evelyn, 87. They arrived at Culpeper having lived full, exciting lives as diplomats and traveling retirees. They were engaged on a political level, first as Socialists and then as Democrats. As a married couple of 62 years, they were an anomaly for the Health Care Center because they were there together and living in the same room.

My sister Heather and I moved them to Culpeper because they were unable to live safely in their four-story townhouse. At first, we hired two, full-time, live-in health-care workers, but the situation proved untenable. When we told Mother and Daddy about our plans, Mother sat up straight on the couch and said, adopting her most forceful persona, "If it's a financial problem, I'll get a job." That moment illustrated her independent steel magnolia character, but for those who knew her she could not be mistaken for who she had been.

For my part, I sequestered my parents in a small, emotional compartment that I opened only when necessary. On this day, my expansive, alternative family—brother and sister singers and other friends—merrily filled my life.

I witnessed the reduction of my vibrant, happy, and intelligent parents as I saw them become people who dimly resembled who they had been. Years of work, parenting, friendships, activism, travel, and learning were background shadows in their current existence. They could not call on any memories to sustain them. They were breathing and living but I had no parents, anymore. Those people were no longer in the room.

Before the nursing home, Daddy had been quick to opine that a sense of humor was essential in confronting the aging process. He began offering this adage when the doctors diagnosed his beloved sister, Molly, with Alzheimer's. To make himself feel better, he would remark, "The worst thing you can do about Alzheimer's is talk about it, because then you think you have it yourself."

He displayed a similar light touch and wit about his and Mother's growing forgetfulness. He told amusing stories of their forays to DC's "Social Safeway," so nicknamed because of its reputation as a social cruising location for the younger set, although they probably never knew this. This weekly trip took them across the city in their blue, Chevy Cavalier. Nothing could convince them—well, convince Mother—to avail themselves of the suitable Safeway two blocks from their home. I am not sure why.

These expeditions occupied the better part of each Friday. Mother put together two lists, one for staples and the other for produce and meat. My father fulfilled the first and Mother the second. They met at the checkout line with the two shopping carts. My father retrieved their car and they loaded the groceries into the trunk. The next stop was the liquor store up the street.

One time, they brought home the contents of the French Embassy's grocery carts! They had been loading their car at the same time as the French Embassy staff and somehow the grocery carts got mixed up, although how never became clear. They discovered their mistake only as they unloaded the groceries at their house. They drove two round trips to Safeway that day to rectify the error.

Soon after they purchased the blue, Chevy Cavalier, they misplaced the car in the Safeway parking lot because they could not remember its color. My friend, Sally, told me that she came upon them just as they were in mid-search and she did not think they recognized her when she called out to them. Although they were confused, they accepted her help to find the car and provided the simplest of descriptions. Sally searched each row until she found a new, blue car with temporary plates, which was theirs.

For many years after Daddy retired in 1973, my parents traveled to Greece and England each summer. Greece was their first and favorite foreign service post. I was born there and given the middle name of Penelope to honor the connection. They returned to England because it was Daddy's birthplace.

I took care of their bills and their home while they were away. They were faithful correspondents and they occasionally telephoned, always in the early morning. They would have a list of topics and questions for me, which made calls informational, short, and less expensive. Although my parents had achieved a comfortable financial status, they continued to spend frugally. They had met during the Depression and married in 1933. International phone calls were tools for exceptional circumstances.

Mother and Daddy unknowingly traveled with invalid passports in the summer of 1988 when they flew from DC to Athens to London before British immigration authorities observed the expiration date. This unusual situation required several international phone calls to Heather, who had the government connections to handle this type of problem.

On their penultimate summer trip in 1990, I arrived at their home in plenty of time for the 30-mile drive to Dulles Airport. Their organizational skills honed over the years had easily met all demands of international airline departures.

Yet, disarray greeted me. They were not ready. I sat for a bit and then realizing that they were getting close to being late for their plane, I offered to help. Their two suitcases rested on their double bed but my parents were reeling around the room without purpose or plan.

Mother suggested I could close the one, big, Samsonite. I looked inside. I did not see any clothing. Instead, the suitcase was full of books, food, towels, and other sundries. I thought about questioning the contents, but figured they would be okay and could buy whatever they had left behind. I shut the suitcase without comment and soon we were on our way to the airport. It was then or never, I figured.

Three weeks later, I received a letter from Daddy. It was a harbinger of the times to come. The letter, whose path was hard to follow, contained duplicates of various passages and what looked like a rewrite of another portion. His handwriting had always been spidery, slanted to the right and difficult to decipher, and he could never spell simple words. I had concluded that he developed this handwriting style because it hid basic spelling errors. He quit school at age 14 and was a self-made man from then on.

He wrote with specific reference to the strange suitcase they had taken along:

> *You, however, must have been the only one who knew how much of our intended material for a two-month trip was lying on our bed or other convenient pieces of furniture in the bedroom. We*

discovered the situation when we opened our bag in our room in Athens. The one from which you can see the 'Acropolis.' No electric shaver, no substitute of course, only a few socks (most of the wrong colors) not for sale anywhere. Fortunately, as we have been putting our belongs [sic] in place, we found some articles we had not included so we thought, "such confusion."... By the way, not included was our bedroom clock, which for many years has risen us from our slumbers.... I've never had such pre-holiday confusion. (Letter from DAS to JPS, dated July 10, 13, & 15, 1990)

They returned to Washington, DC, with no further mishaps or at least with no tales that they were willing to share.

My parents' move to the nursing home in the autumn of 1993 resulted from my mother's traumatic fall and her month's long stay in the hospital. It was the correct decision, but my pain around their altered lives took over my daily life and I could not concentrate on anything. Laughter did not exist during this time. To balance my inner turbulence, I repeatedly reminded myself that things could be much worse; I could be living in Bosnia, for example. I reasoned that my mother and father had sufficient resources. They would be safe in the new place with 24/7 supervision.

There is nothing that can prepare children to lose their parents. Knowing that mine were old and that they could not live forever did not make their mental and physical disintegration tolerable or any less difficult.

On this day, as Fred and I pulled up in Golda, I was happy. I was about to enjoy a period of luxurious inattention to my parents' needs. I would not return for a couple of weeks and there would be no phoning from the road. Pulling into the parking lot of the nursing home always evoked memories of loss, quickly followed by relief. Parking meant I was carrying out my filial duty and that it would soon be time to leave. No visit lasted very long. Fred's presence would make this visit easier than usual. He had met my parents and knew them through my stories. His gregariousness was a boon and he had no qualms about visiting them in the nursing home. A special friend, he always lifted me up.

Fred engaged Mother in chit chat and I joined them. In her illness, her conversation had assumed a predictable, smooth formula, honed by years as a gracious foreign service wife. A glimpse of her personality still made it through, reflected in her respect for manners, which she had instilled in me as a child. In her response to people, especially men, she always thanked her guests for coming and suggested getting together again soon. She concluded each visit by saying, "Will you come for tea sometime?" I imagined Mother moving away down a tunnel—her light ever dimmer.

Two years earlier, Mother had a calamitous fall and her subsequent rescue by the medical profession altered my parents' lives completely. She had fallen on the sidewalk outside their home and had laid unconscious in the dark night until a neighbor found her close to death. Both Mother and Daddy had written Do Not Resuscitate Orders (DNR) but Daddy was not sufficiently cognizant to assist the emergency personnel. Since Heather and I were both out of town at locations unknown to our parents, the DNR was ignored and Mother's life was saved. Her new life was the beginning of a life that neither she nor Daddy wanted and its possibility had always terrified them.

Since then, Mother's ability to recognize her visitors had become unreliable. Sometimes we were her daughters, but she could be equally sure we were cousins, uncles, or caring friends. "No one told me I had daughters," she would say. This version of my mother talked about age, although she could not remember her own. We discussed her age, Daddy's age, and our ages—followed by a revisiting of the same topic. She asked about the age of her own long-dead mother.

It puzzled me to figure out a response, although I came to understand that my answer was more painful to me than to her. I had never met my maternal grandmother Freida. Honesty brought no clarity. I tried by saying, "Mother, Grandmother is not alive, but she would be over 100 now." Mother often followed with another question: "Have you seen her lately?" Or a concern would come to her, "Mother works hard right now. I don't know where she goes."

On this visit, while seated in a wheelchair, Mother showed her appreciation that Fred and I had stopped in on our way out of town. This was basic courtesy—to know the whereabouts of her children, even though she did not know she had daughters. On that occasion, I doubted that she recognized my relationship to her. She might have thought Fred and I were dating but since I had rarely confided in her about my private life, her lack of knowledge about any romantic aspects was not something for which I held her accountable, then or now.

Daddy was lying on a bed. I croaked "hello" to him and then ignored him for the rest of the visit. Once voluble and sociable, Daddy could no longer communicate. Despite coaching from a therapist, he would emit only garbled, audible sounds and if asked to repeat, he could not. Relating to him was a challenge that was much harder than relating to Mother and it was a challenge I could no longer manage and Fred did not tackle.

Daddy had left behind a potential career as a professional cricketer in England to come to the US in 1926. He was a natural athlete and played soccer and tennis as well. Now, he brought to my mind a big, injured bird or, because of his astonishing volume of white hair, an idiot from a Russian novel. I applied his suggestion about drawing on humor but it failed for his situation.

Daddy never realized he was living in Virginia, a state for which he reserved complete disdain by virtue of his activist politics. When the Democrats lost control of the US House of Representatives in 1994, it was a relief that he was unaware. He died without knowing that his son-in-law was no longer the Speaker of the House.

My parents' lives shrunk to this small room with two hospital beds and two wheelchairs, and now, Daddy did not recognize me. His face lit up when others entered the room but he registered no expression when I arrived. The elderly experts, such as the social workers at the Health Care Center, suggested that I not interpret such encounters, but I was not capable of setting aside my hurt feelings. Daddy and I had a difficult falling out when I came out as a Lesbian and since then, our interactions had degraded and almost disappeared.

To wind down from the nursing home and to rev up for the trip ahead, Fred and I stopped at the nearby Golden Corral restaurant. It was the first and last steakhouse of our trip, only acceptable for this meal because it included a salad bar and it was close to our route. There were miles to cover before catching any shuteye, and the next day would be longer and happier.

At dinner, I welcomed being honest with Fred. My memory retains a summary of what I said to him.

> *I wish they were dead. Perhaps it's shocking to say, but it is how I feel. They are not in physical pain, but their lives are no longer their lives. Their lives are sustained by overzealous, excellent health care and good nutrition. They no longer have a say in their lives, and we prolonged their lives by bringing them here. Meanwhile, who they are is not what they were. It's not right for them to have no memory, no joy in remembering, and no hope for life to be better.*

A rule of life occurred to me at the Golden Corral: Never visit your elderly parents when they are resting in bed. They appear frailer and more translucent.

Fred and I made a punctual 8 pm departure from the restaurant and I was ready to drive. "Have Lesbian, will travel," said Fred, as I steered Golda away from our parking spot.

☾   ☾   ☾

Fred with a parting gift from the LGCW, 1985

Photograph of Jane and Me, 2018

Thoughtfulness is your
saving my place in the book
we read together.
(Haiku, JPS 2019)

Happy Me, Athens, Greece, c. 1952

LIST OF PHOTOGRAPHS

ACKNOWLEDGEMENTS
AND THANKS

THIS BOOK is an in-person collaboration of many people and a collaboration of people's voices captured in letters and journals.

Friends who got me started: Martin Blank, Robert Convery, Jane Hoffman, Paul Preston, and Doug Yeuell
Editors: Daniel Weaver, Robert Convery, and Kathy Hendrix
Cover and Interior Design: Glen Edelstein, Hudson Valley Book Design
Art for Back Cover: Kent Gay
Copy Editor and Proofreader: Deborah Weiner

Many friends had the courage to read unfinished portions and offered their encouragement and suggestions. Thanks go to them for their willingness to read my writing in the raw, so to speak. Mark Bowman, Cathie Brettschneider, Lynne J. Brown, Christopher Buckle, A. Peter Burleigh, Regina Carlow, Bryan Dalton, Heather S. Foley, Fred Fishman, C. Paul Heins, Susan Heyward, Omar Hendrix, Jane Hoffman, Steve Holloway, Coy Ludwig, Gerald Mager, Gabrielle Maya, Alvin Mayes, Theresa Moller, Scott Mooney, Amy Moore, Mike Oligmueller, Paul Preston, E. Bryan Samuel, Mark Savad, Dave Strachan, Libby Taylor, Michael Vreeland, Bobbie Weaver, Eugenia Yeuell

Manuscript Readers: Hannah Jacobson Blumenfeld, Beth Boland, Elizabeth Herbert Cottrell, Misti French, Karen McCluskey, Paul Preston, and Doug Yeuell
Consultants on days in Cairo: Peter C. Biella and Joan Biella

ABOUT THE AUTHOR

JILL P. STRACHAN left behind successful grant writing for the pleasures of creating nonfiction, traveling with her partner, playing tennis,
and walking her dog. Her career in arts and association management
spanned 40 years. She holds a Ph.D. in the History of Religion and sings
in Not What You Think, an a cappella group offering songs of social
justice.

CPSIA information can be obtained
at www.ICGtesting.com
Printed in the USA
BVHW040055291021
620154BV00004B/14